In her introduction to the 1957 edition of The Thirty Years' War, historian C.V. Wedgwood acknowledges that her treatment of the war in the original 1938 edition was coloured by the grim mood of the 1930s, and that 'the preoccupations of that unhappy time cast their shadows over its pages'. However, she adds that 'nothing has happened in the relevant fields of research during the last twenty years to make me change my views on the war as a whole.'

More than sixty years later, she would undoubtedly be delighted that scholarship around the Thirty Years' War has moved on dramatically, and in this volume of papers the speakers at the 2018 Helion conference offer a variety of insights into the depth and direction of that progression, with particular reference to the war's effect on the British Isles, the careers of the officers from its shores who participated in the conflict, and the 'trickle-down' effect of the war into the military thinking and technology of those isles.

Keynote speaker Professor Steve Murdoch examines the changes in understanding of British military participation in the Thirty Years' War from a once unsophisticated and dismissive approach to a more enriched and interesting field of study. Where once soldiers operating in the European theatre were crudely dismissed as low ranking, low status, and ultimately ineffective mercenaries, Prof. Murdoch reviews the plethora of work on the subject that has adopted a less sweeping and more critical analysis. He introduces new areas of study including the common soldiery, women and warfare, and medical provision in the conflict.

Military theory, distributed in the form of treatises and manuals, was a rapidly developing field at the time. Keith Dowen examines the work of Catholic Irish colonel Gerat Barry, which has been largely overlooked, reassessing Barry's military career and his Discourse of Military Discipline within the wider context of the Eighty Years' War and contemporary military practice. He also appraises Barry's role in the Irish Rebellion of 1641 and the challenges he and his fellow commanders faced in adapting to a very different kind of war than that which they had previously experienced.

Soldiers who thoroughly understood and successfully practised the military theory and – perhaps like Barry – were also adaptable in their methods, could find ample and extremely varied opportunities abroad during the Thirty Years' War. Michał Paradowski looks into the careers of three officers from the British Isles who fought abroad – Englishman Arthur Aston Jr, Irishman James (Jacob) Butler and Scotsman James (Jacob) Murray – who served in the armies of kings Sigismund III and Władysław IV Vasa between 1621 and 1634 against Cossacks (Butler), Muscovites (Butler and Murray) and Swedes (all three), in Muscovy, Courland, Prussia and on the Baltic coast.

Professor Martyn Bennett also examines military high command during the period, but in England rather than Scotland. He explores the process of appointment of the rival command structures in 1642, at the start of the English Civil Wars: considering how the king and parliament went about choosing the appointees to command in the field armies and the regional commands during the summer and winter of 1642, and who they chose to command their armies and resources as war loomed. The paper posits some suggestions as to the success or otherwise of the attempt to win the war.

Creating a military structure was not merely about field tactics and choosing commanders, however. It included the employment of specialists where required, and David Flintham – whose paper discusses the bringing of Dutch engineers into England during the Civil Wars – demonstrates that the use of foreign experts was nowhere more marked than in the field of military engineering. He considers the foreign, especially Dutch, influence on English fortification during the period, the methods employed and those who practised them. In particular he considers the techniques of this 'Dutch school' on Oxford and King's Lynn.

Fortification was not the only practical military aspect heavily influenced by the war on the Continent. When England went to war to confront the rebellion in Scotland in 1639 it raised its first full field army for nearly half a century, while Europe had been at war for twenty years. In the conference's final paper Stephen Ede-Borrett examines contemporary vexillology, and how much the Thirty Years' War influenced the military flags used by the English Armies from 1639 to 1651.

Serena Jones is the author of *No Armour But Courage: Colonel Sir George Lisle, 1615–1648*, and delivered a paper on Lisle and military professionalism at the 2016 Helion English Civil War Conference; she also edited the collected conference papers for that year (*A New Way of Fighting: Professionalism in the English Civil War*) and for the 2017 conference (*Home and Away: The British Experience of War 1618–1721*). A professional editor, she edits for Helion and also runs her own publishing business, making primary seventeenth-century texts available for modern researchers.

'BRITAIN TURNED GERMANY':
THE THIRTY YEARS' WAR AND ITS IMPACT ON THE BRITISH ISLES 1638–1660

'BRITAIN TURNED GERMANY': THE THIRTY YEARS' WAR AND ITS IMPACT ON THE BRITISH ISLES, 1638-1660

Proceedings of the 2018 Helion & Company 'Century of the Soldier' Conference

---

Edited by Serena Jones

Helion & Company Limited

Helion & Company Limited
Unit 8 Amherst Business Centre
Budbrooke Road
Warwick
CV34 5WE
England
Tel. 01926 499 619
Email: info@helion.co.uk
Website: www.helion.co.uk
Twitter: @helionbooks
Visit our blog at http://blog.helion.co.uk/

Published by Helion & Company 2019
Designed and typeset by Serena Jones
Cover designed by Paul Hewitt, Battlefield Design (www.battlefield-design.co.uk)
Printed by Jellyfish Solutions (www.jellyfishsolutions.co.uk)

ISBN 978-1-912866-62-5

British Library Cataloguing-in-Publication Data.
A catalogue record for this book is available from the British Library.

Contents

List of Figures

List of Contributors

Professor Steve Murdoch
Professor Steve Murdoch is a specialist on British involvement in the Thirty Years' War and is based at the University of St Andrews. He has published widely on the subject, most recently co-authoring (with Alexia Grosjean) the monograph *Alexander Leslie and the Scottish Generals of the Thirty Years' War* (Brill, 2014) and a range of articles on the war covering subjects a diverse as 'Letters home from a common soldier' (2015) to 'Medical Provision' among the British Regiments in Swedish and Dutch service (2017). His other major works include the award-winning works *The Terror of the Seas? Scottish Maritime Warfare, 1513-1713* (Brill, 2010) and *Network North: Scottish Kin, Commercial and Covert Associations in Northern Europe, 1603-1746* (Brill, 2006).

Keith Dowen
Keith Dowen is the Assistant Curator of European Armour at the Royal Armouries specialising in late 16th and 17th century arms and armour. He has lectured widely on the arms and armour of the period and has published a number of articles on the subject including a study of buff coats in the 2015 edition of the *Journal of the Arms and Armour Society*. He is currently in the process of writing the Royal Armouries guide to the arms and armour of the British Civil Wars.

Michał Paradowski
Michał Paradowski is an independent Polish researcher, living in Scotland. While interested in both 16th and 17th century warfare, his main fields of study are Polish-Swedish wars waged between 1621 and 1635. He has published historical articles in Polish, English, Russian and French; also a book (in Polish), 'Studies and Materials regarding wars against Sweden 1600-1635' (Napoleon V, 2013). In his spare time he works as historical editor for Polish publishing house Napoleon V and is historical consultant for the 'By Fire and Sword' miniature game produced by Wargamer Games Studio Ltd. His historical blog can be found at <http://kadrinazi.blogspot.co.uk/>.

Professor Martyn Bennett
Professor Bennett was born in Bridlington, educated at the Joseph Rowntree School outside York, and has lived in Loughborough for over forty years. He has worked on the civil war in Britain and Ireland for over thirty years. He has published over a dozen books and numerous articles on the war and has most recently published a study of Cromwell's military achievements which has analysed the nature of his genius. Professor Bennett is the Professor of Early Modern History at Nottingham Trent University and a broadcaster who presents a documentary series about the history of Nottinghamshire for Notts TV: Rediscovering Notts.

David Flintham FRGS
David Flintham is a military historian specialising in 17th century fortress warfare. He is the author of three books, and has contributed to two others. He has also written nearly 50 published essays and articles. A fellow of the Royal Geographical Society, he is on the committee of the Fortress Study Group, and is project manager of the King's Lynn Under Siege ECW archaeological project. He is currently writing two further books for Helion, both with an ECW fortress-warfare theme. Although London-based, David still dreams of a Scottish Six Nations Grand Slam. See also <http://www.vauban.co.uk/>.

Stephen Ede-Borrett
Stephen Ede-Borrett has been fascinated by military flags for nearly half a century and in that time has contributed numerous papers to a number of journals including *Flagmaster*, the journal of the Flag Institute, and the *Flag Bulletin*, the journal of the Flag Research Center, both of which organisations he has held membership of. He is the author of *The Army of James II for* Helion and is also currently Honorary Chairman of the Pike and Shot Society and a member of a number of other historical societies. His other major interests are movies, international cricket, superhero comics and the cats that allow him and his partner Mary to share their home. He lives in what he considers to be the greatest City on the planet – London. He maintains he is not at all biased in that opinion.

Introduction

Serena Jones

The theme for Helion's 2018 Century of the Soldier conference, and thus the title for this volume of papers, 'Britain Turned Germany', is a play on the title of Ian Roy's paper 'England turned Germany? The Aftermath of the Civil War in its European Context', presented at the Royal Historical Society's conference in 1977.[1] Roy discusses the British view of the violence of the Thirty Years' War (1618–48), and the 'horror stories from Germany' being disseminated by the British press as civil war loomed in the British Isles. In particular they focused on the popular terror of the 'Plundering Soldier', who was 'chillingly described as feeding on the entrails of the kingdom'; as the war developed, Parliamentarian propaganda readily identified this figure with Royalist soldiers – many of whom had undertaken military service on the Continent – and in particular with Prince Rupert, the King's half-German nephew.

> The London press and pulpits highlighted atrocities committed by mercenaries trained, they believed, in a bloody school of war. The sack of West Country towns by Rupert, in an early campaign, was a case of 'England turned Ireland', according to one account. It seemed certain that, as the war progressed, England would turn Germany.[2]

However, Roy continues, this threat of parallel violence did not materialise: 'On the whole, analogies between the Civil War and contemporaneous warfare in the continent have been rejected [by historians], if considered at all.' Whilst retrospective analysis of the period considers that the degree of violence during the English Civil Wars may not have attained the heights contemporaries feared – with a few arguable exceptions – the war on the Continent did, nevertheless, draw in the British Isles militarily, and as Roy states:

> After 1638 there was a constant, if not large-scale, two-way traffic in arms and men between all regions of the British conflict and the continent. The European powers continued to

1 Published in *Transactions of the Royal Historical Society*, vol. 28 (1978), pp.127–144.
2 Roy, 'England Turned Germany', p.128.

> recruit for their armies in Britain, while allowing some of their own commanders, particularly the British among them, to return home, often with fellow officers and followers.
>
> Not only the Cavaliers ... but the Roundheads benefited from this influx of foreign or foreign-trained military talent.[3]

As Professor Steve Murdoch notes in his keynote paper, thanks to new scholarship the extent of British influence on and participation in the Thirty Years' War is becoming apparent, contrary to previous contentions. Fresh research is uncovering the role of British commanders from all parts of the British Isles, and the private soldiers they raised at home and took abroad. Motivations for service were manifold, ranging from confessional beliefs to supporting King James's daughter Elizabeth and her husband Frederick V of the Palatinate, ejected from Bohemia in 1620. As Professor Murdoch sets out, English and Scottish officers and regiments in particular played a significant role throughout the war.

However, as Roy says, the British–Continental military efforts very much two-way. Keith Dowen offers us the career of Irishman Gerat Barry, who served in Flanders with the Spanish army during the Eighty Years' War with the United Provinces. Barry went on to write *A Discourse in Military Discipline*, then took his wealth of experience back to Ireland, fighting for the Confederates; although not always with success, for the military factors Barry was familiar with in Flanders were not replicated across the Channel. Yet the Continental military methods of Barry and his fellow officers left a lasting mark on the organisation of Confederate soldiery. Michał Paradowski presents three more British officers who plied their trade in Europe, principally in Polish service: Arthur Aston (Jr), James Butler, and James Murray, respectively English, Irish and Scottish. All periodically returned home to find recruits and materiel. Whilst Murray became a naval specialist for the Poles, Aston returned to Britain at the outbreak of the English Civil War, exploiting his knowledge of the new art of dragoon warfare in the service of Charles I.

Professor Martyn Bennett's paper also brings us back to Britain and specifically to the Civil War, considering a selection of the senior commanders on each side, their backgrounds and careers, and examining how the particular command structures of King and Parliament developed. This process, and its results, were of course unique to British circumstances, and social status played a large part in the selection of commanders; nonetheless, a large proportion of these key figures had garnered some kind of prior military experience abroad, and like Gerat Barry would have brought this to bear on one side or other in the British crisis. In this respect Roy offers also the example of James King, the Earl of Newcastle's deputy, 'a Scots officer of great experience'; and on the Parliamentarian side, of Joseph Wagstaffe, commander of Hampden's Foot, who had been in French service.[4] Although outside the scope of Professor Bennett's paper, we

3 Roy, p.131.
4 *Ibid.*

might also recall the large number of middle- and lower-ranking British commissioned officers who had also served abroad in some capacity; and also the large number of foreign officers who had come to Britain specifically to offer their services to her King or Parliament, just as Barry, Aston, Butler, Murray and their like had previously offered their swords to Charles's counterparts abroad.

Of course, military expertise was not confined to the physical act of fighting, and our final two papers, from David Flintham and Stephen Ede-Borrett, examine technical aspects of warfare – respectively, fortifications and flags – the theories and practices of which, like the tactics and techniques brought back by Barry and Aston, became interwoven into British military thinking. Sieges were a fundamental part of Continental warfare, and defensive fortifications at this period were highly advanced. David Flintham gives a detailed overview of the field as it stood at the time of the Thirty Years' War, and of the key figures in it, and in particular assesses the influence of Dutch fortification methods on English works during the Civil War period. Roy notes that 'the Dutch influence was predominant', and that Colonel Charles Lloyd, 'whose waterworks transformed Oxford into an impregnable fortress, and who rebuilt the defences of Devizes in the latest style, had mapped the famous siege of Maastricht ten years before.'[5]

Military colours of the period, unlike fortifications, have no suite of contemporary designers or experts to inform us of their initial development or later use. Captain Thomas Venn, who described the English system of 'differencing' colours prior to the Restoration, only did so in 1672 and then only as part of a broader military work. The system is consequently named after him, but Stephen Ede-Borrett, in our final paper, theorises in detail that the system in fact originated on the Continent.

'Britain turned Germany'? In terms of violence, it seems largely not. Yet in respect of developing military technique and technology there is no mistaking the influence the Continental wars had on those of the British Isles, and it was just that, *Continental* influence, not merely German: the cumulative experience of conflict in Dutch, French, Spanish, Swedish, and other territories seeped inexorably back into Britain through the exchange of military 'professionals', combative and technical alike, and the experiences of those private men who fought abroad and had the good fortune to return home. The press also played its part in disseminating these experiences in the form of news, and printing them in book form for the purposes of instruction. The situation was self-reinforcing: experiences encountered abroad were taken home, to influence and instruct a new wave of military 'professionals' who would hire themselves out and re-export their expertise to the Continent. Undoubtedly the same situation occurred in reverse, with Continental officers serving in the British Isles, and bringing British experience, perspectives, and even techniques, back across the Channel.

5 Roy, p.132. Lloyd was Royalist governor of Devizes in 1645.

Nicrina ad Heroas Anglos. An overview of the British and the Thirty Years' War

Professor Steve Murdoch

The Thirty Years' War is generally taken to refer to the series of European conflicts that took place between 1618 and 1648. In truth, some of these had a much older pedigree, most importantly the Dutch conflict with Spain, later known as the Eighty Years' War (1568–1648) of which the last 30 years overlapped with what contemporary Britons called the 'German Warres'. Other conflicts rumbled on for years after 1648, most notably the Franco-Spanish War (1634–1659). Thus, although the terminology concerning the duration of the war can seem anachronistic, yet it was nevertheless a contemporary term used in several pamphlets in and after 1648. The conflicts engulfed Europe and at various points engaged almost every European kingdom, duchy and city-state in some way or another.

The war began in 1618 when the Protestant nobles of Bohemia rejected Ferdinand II of Austria as their elected monarch and threw his representatives out of the window in the famous 2nd defenestration of Prague. Those thrown from the window survived, but there would be severe consequences thereafter. Ferdinand became Holy Roman Emperor in 1619, the same year that the Bohemians elected Frederick V of the Palatinate as their new king. With Frederick as leader of the Protestant Union (a loose coalition that involved much of reformed Europe), and Ferdinand now at the head of the conglomerate Holy Roman Empire which nominally had control over some of the Protestant Union, the scene was set for a clash of dynastic, religious and political ideas that would go on for the next three decades. There is no need in this article to go into every aspect of every theatre of the war. These have been covered in numerous general histories of the conflict.[1]

1 * The author wishes to express his thanks to Jack Abernethy, Alexia Grosjean, Helmer Helmers and Simon Marsh for their comments and help with finding the sources used in the preparation of this chapter. Any errors deriving from them are, of course, my own.

Rather, the focus here will be firmly on the interventions from Great Britain both at state and private level. Work in the field is uneven, with Scotland having received the greatest coverage, concerning both those fighting for and those against the Hapsburg Empire.[2] The only sustained piece of research on English military participation is the doctoral dissertation of Adam Marks.[3] Most other English scholarship tends to focus on the reception of the conflict in England through contemporary English language texts.[4] Indeed, discussion of any British participation is usually quite dismissive or wholly fails to understand the sheer scale of that involvement.

Motivation for participation in either side was informed by a number of relevant factors including dynastic loyalty, national pride, confessional allegiance, the expectations of kin groups and coercion among others.[5] Some simply fought for financial remuneration and a few merely for adventure. Yet for the vast majority of the 120,000 or more British soldiers who joined in the conflict on the anti-Habsburg side, it was an amalgam of these which brought them to the 'German Wars', as summed up neatly by Colonel Robert Monro:

> I did come at it [the war]; for many reasons, but especially for the libertie of the daughter of our dread Soveraigne, the distressed Queen of Bohemia, and her Princlie Issue; next for the libertie of our distressed brethren in Christ.[6]

1 Grand overviews tend to miss the important nuances of the participants in the conflict. Excellent editions with vastly different emphasis include J.V. Polišenský, *The Thirty Years' War* (London: Batsford, 1971); Peter Wilson, *Europe's Tragedy: A New History of the Thirty Years War* (London: Penguin edition, 2010). The literature available in other languages is too extensive to list here.

2 To select only two works looking at the most influential commanders see David Worthington, *Scots in Habsburg Service, 1618–1648* (Leiden: Brill, 2004); Steve Murdoch and Alexia Grosjean, *Alexander Leslie and the Scottish Generals of the Thirty Years' War, 1618–1648* (London: Pickering & Chatto, 2014).

3 Adam Marks, 'England, the English and the Thirty Years' War, 1618–1648' (unpublished PhD thesis, University of St Andrews, 2012). Older works focussing on the earlier part of the Dutch Eighty Years' War include near hagiographical works like C.R. Markham, *"The Fighting Veres": Lives of Sir Francis Vere, general of the queen's forces in the Low Countries, governor of the Brill and of Portsmouth, and of Sir Horace Vere, general of the English forces in the Low Countries, governor of the Brill, master-general of ordnance, and Baron Vere of Tilbury* (London: Sampson Low et al. Ltd, 1888).

4 For the literary analysis see Barbara Donagan, 'Halcyon Days and the Literature of War: England's Military Education before 1642', *Past & Present*, No. 147 (May 1995), pp.65–100; Jayne E.E. Boys, *London's News Press and the Thirty Years' War* (Woodbridge: The Boydell Press, 2010), pp.65–91; Kirsty Rolfe, '"Now published for the satisfaction of every true English heart": The war over the Palatinate, Protestant identity, and subjecthood in British pamphlets, 1620–26' (unpublished PhD thesis, UCL, 2014).

5 An excellent starting point for confessional motivation for Protestants remains David Trim, 'Calvinist Internationalism and the English Officer Corps, 1562–1642', *History Compass* 4/6 (2006), pp.1024–1048; Donagan, 'Halcyon Days', pp.73–74.

6 Robert Monro, *His Expedition with a worthy Scots Regiment called Mackeyes* (2 Parts, London: William Iones, 1637), II, pp. 61–62.

When Frederick V became King of Bohemia, his wife – Princess Elizabeth Stuart – now became the Queen of Bohemia. This iconic Fife-born daughter of King James VI proved the main totem for attracting Britons into the Continental armies fighting for the restoration of the Palatinate and Bohemia. Her fortunes and those of her children were naturally of great concern to the House of Stuart, but also to her German relatives and her blood uncle, Christian IV of Denmark–Norway. From the outset patriotic British broadsheets, poets and authors publicised their hopes for Elizabeth whom they proclaimed to be 'The Jewell of Europe'.[7] The Aberdonian poet Arthur Johnston's two poems *Saravicto to Biomea* and *Biomea to Saravicto* set up a mythical dialogue between the characters 'Austria' and 'Bohemia' to enlighten the British literati of the root causes of the conflict.[8] More overtly, he directly challenged them in his poem *Nicrina ad Heroas Anglos* to remember the previous glories of that nation, especially those victories of the earls of Vere, Oxford and Essex – all combatants in the struggle to recover the Palatinate.[9] Yet while directing his title to the 'Heroes of England', Johnson was careful throughout only to talk of Britain and the British, reminding his audience that even if the places under threat from the 'Imperial Eagle' were not worthy of their involvement, the person of Elizabeth Stuart was. Poet John Taylor was equally careful to emphasise both the importance of the Palatine house and the British role in defending it in his poem, *The subjects [sic] joy for Parliament*.[10] After all, as Adam Marks succinctly put it, 'to defend Frederick was to defend an Englishman, and to defend Elizabeth to defend a Scot', making the Palatinate campaigns a thoroughly British affair.[11] The martial classes, reacting to poetical provocation and polemical encouragement through broadsheets and corantos, became involved in a far more belligerent way than often historically understood.

While continuing complex diplomatic negotiations with both Protestant and Catholic powers, King James facilitated a number of militarily initiatives. Already owning five English and Scottish regiments employed in Dutch service he could swiftly move professional veterans to Bohemia without worrying about the cost of levying and training them.[12] James had done this previously during the War of

7 Thomas Kellie, *Pallas Armata or Militarie Instructions for the Learned* (Edinburgh: The aires of Andro Hart, 1627), p.2a; Monro, *His Expedition*, I, p.37.

8 The two poems found (with editorial) in Arthur Johnson, *Musa Latina Aberdonensis* (3 vols., Aberdeen: Spalding Club, 1892), I, pp. 53–75.

9 Johnson, *Musa Latina Aberdonensis,* I, pp.76–85.

10 John Taylor, *The subjects joy for Parliament* (London: Edward All-de, 1621).

11 Adam Marks, 'Recognizing Friends from Foes: Stuart Politics, English Military Networks and Alliances with Denmark and the Palatinate', in Valentina Caldari and Sara J. Wolfson (eds.), *Stuart Marriage Diplomacy: Dynastic Politics in their European Context, 1604–1630* (Woodbridge: Boydell Press, 2018), p.180. Frederick and any future children of his were naturalised as English on 16 April 1613.

12 For the Scots (formed 1572) see James Ferguson (ed.), *Papers Illustrating the History of the Scots Brigade in the Service of the United Netherlands* (3 vols., Edinburgh: Scottish History Society, 1899–1901), vol.1. For the origins of the Anglo-Dutch Brigade (formed 1582) see David Trim 'Fighting "Jacob's Wars":

the Jülich Succession (1610) in support of his Protestant allies.[13] In so doing James deployed the first known British-flagged army in history, with Scots and Englishmen serving together under the command of General Sir Edward Cecil, seconded by Colonel Sir Robert Henderson. They were in British flag, pay and under British military jurisdiction for the duration of the campaign.

In 1610, 1614 and 1620, the British units in Dutch service were available to James due to the 12-year truce then in place between Spain and the Dutch Republic (1609–1621). Thus in 1620 some 1,000 soldiers of the Scots–Dutch brigade under Colonel John Seton's command were sent to protect Elizabeth Stuart in Bohemia.[14] Subsequently, the Scottish Catholic, Sir Andrew Gray, returned from Prague to recruit more soldiers for Frederick V.[15] His 'Regiment of Britons' composed of 1,500 Scots and 1,000 Englishmen set sail for the Continent in May 1620.[16] Two months after Gray departed, Sir Horace Vere's English regiment also set out for the Continent, though some 500 deserted after a quarrel with their officers over pay and conditions.[17] The main armies never arrived in time to participate in the Battle of White Mountain which had proved disastrous for the Protestant army under Frederik V, albeit Sir William Waller and Elizabeth's lifeguard arrived in time to escort the royals away from Prague.[18] Nevertheless, Gray's forces held onto one Bohemian town until January 1621, but after three major assaults, departed Bohemia to join the English forces occupying Heidelberg, Frankenthal and Mannheim.[19] The

The Employment of English and Welsh Mercenaries in the European Wars of Religion: France and the Netherlands, 1562–1610' (PhD dissertation, King's College, University of London, 2002).

13 See *Resolutiën der Staten-Generaal: Nieuwe Reeks 1610–1670. Deel I, 1610–1612 edited by Arie Theodorus van Deursen* (The Hague:Nijhoff, 1971), pp. 44–45, 60, 99 and 167. Resolutions 246, 249, 331, 534 and 919. Variously dated between 26 February and 3 July 1610. These are discussed in Steve Murdoch, 'James VI and the formation of a Stuart British Military Identity' in Steve Murdoch and Andrew Mackillop (eds.), *Fighting for Identity: Scottish Military Experience, c.1550–1900* (Leiden: Brill, 2002), pp.12–15.

14 J.V. Polišenský, *Tragic Triangle: The Netherlands, Spain and Bohemia 1617–1621* (Prague: Univerzita Karlova, 1991), p.181; Polišenský, *The Thirty Years' War*, pp.125–126.

15 Gray's commission from Frederick V is found in S.R. Gardiner (ed.), *Letters and other documents illustrating relations between England and Germany at the commencement of the Thirty Years' War, 1619–1620* (London: Camden Society, 1868), p.143. Frederick V to King James, 16/26 January 1620; *Calendar of State Papers, Domestic series [CSPD], of the reign of James I, vol. 10. 1619–1623* edited by Mary Anne Everett Green (London: Longman, 1858), p.125. 26 February 1620; Swedish Riksarkivet [hereafter SRA], Anglica V, Sir James Spens to Chancellor Axel Oxenstierna, and same to Gustav II Adolf, both dated 20 April 1620.

16 *Register of the Privy Council of Scotland, vol. XII, 1619–1622* (Edinburgh: General Register House, 1895), lxxviii; *Calendar of State Papers Relating to English Affairs in the Archives of Venice*, Volume 16, 1619–1621. (His Majesty's Stationery Office: London, 1910), pp.262–263. Girolamo Lando to Venice, 28 May 1620.

17 John Taylor, *Taylor his Trauels: From the Citty of London in England, to the Citty of Prague in Bohemia* (London: Nicholas Okes, 1620) B4; Anon., *Certaine Letters declaring in part the passage of affaires in the palatinate from September to the present moneth of April* (Amsterdam: I.B., April 1621), A4, B2-B3; Steve Murdoch, *Britain, Denmark–Norway and the House of Stuart, 1603–1660* (East Linton: Tuckwell Press, East Linton, 2003), p.50; Marks, 'Recognizing Friends from Foes', pp.181–183.

18 Barbara Donagan, 'Waller, Sir William' in *ODNB*.

19 Anon., *Certaine Letters*, B3-5; Murdoch, *Britain*, p.51; Marks, 'Recognizing Friends from Foes', pp.181–183.

British troops were thwarted in their hope for relief by the politics of finance then ongoing in England. The English Parliament scuppered an attempt by King James to facilitate a massive relief army of 30,000 men by refusing to fund even 50 percent of the estimated £1,000,000 costs (with 50 percent to be supplied by the King).[20] The English Parliament simply did not see the issues in the same terms as the King and it was they who opposed his plans.[21] Representatives of the English Parliament claimed they wanted stronger action in support of the Palatinate yet seemed to place obstacles in the way of the King's desire to achieve it. Nevertheless, Colonel Seton and his Scots held out in the Bohemian town of Třeboň until 1622, long after Frederick V and his family had retired to the Dutch Republic. Soon after, Sir Horace Vere took a relief force to join Count Mansfeld in the Palatinate, originally destined to amount to 8,000 infantry and 1,600 horse.[22] There were also hopes that Sir Andrew Gray might raise some 6,000 troops to be sent into Cleves, though events would prevent any such levy until January 1625, partially due to Dutch resistance.[23] Unsupported due to political machinations, Vere's Englishmen stubbornly held on in Frankenthal until April 1623. Under a separate agreement made with the Infanta Isabella Clara Eugina (Governor of the Netherlands on behalf of Spain), King James ordered the garrison to retire for a period of 18 months while diplomatic negotiations continued.[24] As Adam Marks has convincingly argued in his detailed discussion of the affair, this was not a surrender, but a limited sequestration which, the English believed, would eventually result in the St George's Cross flying over the city by October 1623 at the latest.[25] Once more the soldiery were let down by the politicians.

For the time being, those who wished to fight the Habsburgs did so through service in other combatant armies. The siege of Bergen-op-Zoom (July to October 1622) saw Colonel James Henderson's Scots once more serve alongside his former commander, General Edward Cecil. The siege proved costly with Henderson being the highest ranked of the numerous Britons killed defending the city. Indeed, he became something of a poster-boy to the Dutch who proclaimed his actions in storming the enemy trenches to be an example to all their officers.[26] Thomas Gainsford reported

20 The costs and the debates are discussed in detail in Marks, 'England', pp.99–101.

21 Michael Roberts, *Gustavus Adolphus: A History of Sweden, 1611–1632*, 2 vols. (London: Longmans, 1953–1958), I, pp.185–186.

22 Danish Rigsarkivet, TKUA, England AII7. Sir Robert Anstruther to Christian Friis *c*.1622. These exact numbers are also recorded in J.A. Worp (ed.), *De Briefwisseling van Constantijn Huygens, Deel I, 1608–1634* (The Hague: Nijhoff, 1911), p.84. Constantijn Huygens to his parents, 7 March 1622. The information probably derived from Anstruther's friend and fellow diplomat James Hay (later Earl of Carlisle).

23 SRA, Oxenstiernska samlingen, E379. James Spens to Axel Oxenstierna, 3 November 1622; Murdoch, *Britain*, pp.55–56.

24 Murdoch, *Britain*, p.57.

25 Marks, 'Recognizing Friends from Foes', pp.182–184.

26 Ferguson, *Scots Brigade*, I, p. 60; See also *Resolutiën der Staten-General: Nieuw Reeks. Deel 6, 1623–1624* edited by J. Roelevink (The Hague: Nijhoff, 1989), pp.36, 40 and 55.

some 600 English and Irish also died in addition to Henderson and his men.[27] Thereafter, the Dutch authorities cynically used Henderson's widow's status as an encouragement to their officers to die like Henderson rather than in their beds. Thus, Anna Kirkpatrick received a generous payout from the States General while many other women were initially denied their pensions.[28] Instead they had to rely on the honouring of wills and testaments carefully crafted by the soldiers in advance of the commencement of hostilities.[29]

In part, due to the sacrifice of numerous Britons, Bergen-op-Zoom remained under the control of the United Provinces. General Edward Cecil and Colonels Horace Vere, Charles Morgan, Edward Harwood, William Brog and Francis Henderson now commanded the six British regiments in Dutch service, an additional English one having been added.[30] They continued to serve the Republic both in garrison and (as a bonus) in a protective role for exiled Stuart–Palatinate court ensconced in The Hague. Throughout 1624 and 1625 a further four English regiments were temporarily brought into Dutch service bringing the British contingent up to 10 full regiments.[31] Their levying coincided with plans by King James to facilitate larger armies designed to move directly into the Holy Roman Empire. Some of these at least would be deployed outside the Republic in proxy wars.

One major British expedition, set to include some 12,000 men, was levied by Count Ernst von Mansfeld in 1624, among whom some 4,000 Scots were expected to be commanded by Sir Andrew Gray.[32] So it was that the composition of the regiments themselves took on a particularly 'British' flavour, being deliberately formed to include Englishmen in Scottish regiments and vice versa. For instance, Lieutenant Robert Douglas took charge of 150 soldiers from Nottinghamshire who were ordered into Sir Andrew Gray's own regiment.[33] Some 200 more Englishmen were also to be delivered to either Captain Archibald Douglas or Captain James Beaton, also officers in Gray's

27 Boys, *London's News Press*, p.128.

28 Steve Murdoch and Zickermann, Kathrin, '"Bereft of all Human Help?": Scottish Widows during the Thirty Years' War (1618–1648)', *Northern Studies*, 50 (2019), pp.119–120.

29 For Scottish cases of common soldiers making wills, sometimes together with their wives as joint testators, see Steve Murdoch, 'The Repatriation of Capital to Scotland: A Case Study of Dutch Testaments and Miscellaneous Notarial Instruments' M. Varricchioed.), *Back to Caledonia* (Edinburgh: Birlinn, 2012), pp.38–57. English cases survive too. In 1620, Salomon Dexter, an English soldier under Colonel John Ogle, made a reciprocal will with his wife, Jannetje Pieters. See Stadsarchief Rotterdam, Notarissente Rotterdam (ONA) 18/102. Testament, 30 March 1620.

30 F.J.G. Ten Raa and F. De Bas, *Het Staatsche Leger 1568–1795: ondertoezicht van den Chef van den Generalen Staf, Deel III,1609–1625* (Breda: Nijhoff, 1915), pp.179–185.

31 These were the regiments of the earls of Essex, Oxford, Willoughby and Southampton. See Ten Raa and De Bas, *Het Staatsche Leger*, III, pp.181–182.

32 Elizabeth Thomson, (ed.), *The Chamberlain Letters: A selection of the letters of John Chamberlain concerning life in England from 1597–1626* (London: John Murray, 1966), pp.333–334, 9 October 1624; *CSPD, vol. 11. 1623–1625,* edited by Mary Anne Everett Green (London: Longman, 1859), pp.397–420. For reporting of the levy in England see Boy's, *London's News Press*, pp.205–206.

33 *CSPD,* vol. 11. 1623–1625, p.413. Lord Lieutenant to the Council, 19 December 1624.

regiment.[34] Thus, the 'Scottish' regiment of Sir Andrew Gray in 1624 contained Scottish officers and men, but also several hundred English recruits. This did not arise out of a shortage of volunteers. One of the four specifically English regiments of Mansfeld's British army was assigned to Colonel James Hay, Viscount Doncaster, the son of the Earl of Carlisle.[35] Though his colonelcy may have been titular and bestowed because of his social rank, nevertheless the English Privy Council records contain warrants for four senior Scottish officers from Doncaster's regiment to press men in England for service in the new British army.[36] At least one of the four 'English' regiments was therefore recruited in the name of, and commanded by Scots.[37] That said, not all were recruited willingly. There were many men who were terrified at being pressed into service. One English report from 1624 concluded:

> Our soldiers are marching on all sides to Dover. God send them good shipping and good success, but such a rabble of raw and poor rascals have not lightly been seen, and go so unwillingly that they must rather be driven than led. You may guess how base we are grown when one that was pressed hung himself for fear or cursed heart, another ran into the Thames, and after much debating with the constable and officers, when he could not be dismissed, drowned himself. Another cut off all his fingers of one hand, and another put out his own eyes with salt.[38]

Echoing the fear of war seen among the English levy, Scots too engaged in self-harm and suicide. Sir George Hay observed in 1627:

> the desperat courses taken this last yeare by manȝe in this land in euerie pairt of the cuntrey yea in our sight in the counsell chambre (manȝe making themselffs away by hanging, stabbing and vther sortes of death; vthers cutting yair lims yat yej micht be onseruiceable) and all for feare to be sent to Germanie.[39]

34 *Acts of the Privy Council of England* [*APC*], *vol. 39,1623–1625* edited by J.V. Lyle (London: HMSO, 1933), p.395. By the 24th of the same month it was made clear in a letter from James VI and I that the men given to Douglas were intended for another company under Captain Thomas Beaton, also of Gray's regiment. See *CSPD*, 1623–1625, p.418. King James to Sir Andrew Gray, 24 December 1624.

35 Rot E. Schreiber, 'The First Carlisle Sir James Hay, First Earl of Carlisle as Courtier, Diplomat and Entrepreneur, 1580–1636', *Transactions of the American Philosophical Society*, Vol. 74, No. 7 (1984), p.135.

36 *APC, vol. 39,1623–1625*, p.398.

37 A number of other Scottish officers waited in Scotland and England for positions in the new Mansfeld army. See *CSPD*, 1623–1625, pp. 464 and 551. Some of these are named as lieutenants John Haitley, George Douglas, James Stewart 'and other officers' who 'having served under Count Mansfeld since the beginning of the Bohemian wars, they came to Scotland to join the new levy'.

38 Thomson (ed.), *The Chamberlain Letters*, pp.337–338. 18 December 1624.

39 National Library of Scotland, Morton Papers, MS 82, no. 32. Sir George Hay (Chancellor of Scotland) to the Earl of Morton, 30 December 1627. With thanks to Dr Aonghas Maccoinnich for this reference.

The tribulations of the recruiting process are self-evident from these two examples. However, they were not the only impairment to getting men onto the Continent. After sailing from Dover on 22 January 1625 the British troops under Mansfeld were refused permission to land in France as originally planned. The reason for the refusal was the nervousness of Louis XIII at the projected arrival of so many armed heretics in his kingdom.[40] There were also problems fulfilling the main levy and it may be that Mansfeld's force totalled only some 10,000 men.[41]

During the long wait at muster in England and aboard ships, many of the English troops succumbed to disease and died in their droves.[42] Contemporary reports certainly contend that conditions aboard their ships were so bad that than many of the soldiers threw themselves into the sea rather than suffer a slow death on board.[43] Yet several thousand of these soldiers eventually landed at Vlissingen in the United Provinces where they expected to be joined by 2,000 cavalry under the Count of Halberstadt in February 1625.[44] Reliable intelligencers noted that Mansfeld's force was immediately split, with 4,000 troops being held back in Zeeland upon arrival. Several thousand more of them moved on to help the Dutch at the siege of Breda, Halberstadt's cavalry joining them in March.[45] They operated alongside the existing English regiments which were already heavily involved on the assault on Terheijden in May as part of the defence of Breda.[46] Originally, King James had forbidden their use as he continued to honour his agreements with Infanta Isabella. However, when Charles I succeeded his father in March, it was argued that previous obligations regarding the use of the troops had died with King James.[47] Thus the Anglo-Dutch regiments were committed to battle under the command of Generals Vere and Oxford. Among their men, young English captains such as William Killigrew, Ferdinando Knightley and John Cromwell

40 SRA, Oxenstiernska samlingen, E577. Ludwig Camerarius to Axel Oxenstierna, no place, 28 January 1625.

41 SRA, Oxenstiernska samlingen, E702. Jan Rutgers to Axel Oxenstierna, The Hague, 11 December 1624. Caution must be exercised. Some scholars cite numbers as high as 15,000 Englishmen arriving in 1625. See Ronald Asch, 'Mansfeld, (Peter) Ernst von, count von Mansfeld' in *ODNB*

42 *APC, vol. 39, 1623–1625*, pp.434–435; *CSPD*, vol. 11. 1623–1625, p.455; F.C. Montague, *The History of England 1603–1660* (London: Longmans, 1907), p.123; Leo Tandrup(ed.), *Svensk agent vedSundet; Toldkommissærog agent iHelsingør. Anders Svenssonsdepecher till Gustav II Adolf og Axel Oxenstierna 1621–1625* (Aarhus: Universitetsforlaget, 1971), pp.546–547. Anders Svensson to Axel Oxenstierna/ Gustav II Adolf, 14 March 1625; C. Russell, *The Crisis of Parliaments: English History 1509–1660* (Oxford: OUP, 1971), p.299.

43 SRA, Oxenstiernska samlingen, E702. Jan Rutgers to Axel Oxenstierna, The Hague, 24 February 1625; Boys, *London's News Press*, p.211.

44 Tandrup, *Svensk agent ved Sundet*, pp.546–547 and pp.550–551. Anders Svensson to Axel Oxenstierna/ Gustav II Adolf, 14 and 31 March 1625; Murdoch, *Britain*, p.60.

45 SRA, Oxenstiernska samlingen, E702. Jan Rutgers to Axel Oxenstierna, The Hague, 24 February and 21 March 1625.

46 Marks, 'England and the English', pp.73–4. See also A.T.S. Goodrick (ed.), *The Relation of Syndam Poyntz, 1624–1636* (London: Royal Historical Society, 1908), p.46.

47 Ten Raa and De Bas, *Het Staatsche Leger*, III, pp.136–137.

were cutting their teeth while Sir Jacob Astley (lieutenant-colonel in Southampton's regiment) was prominent in the action. In total some 62 Englishmen were killed and a further 110 wounded.[48] Despite their efforts, or those of Mansfeld's volunteers, this action failed and soon Breda fell on 5 June 1625 and was reported to the English Parliament within days.[49] This Mansfeld intervention ended with the disbandment of companies or redistribution of troops among the allies. Those of Viscount Doncaster and others were to be loaned back to the King of Great Britain for service elsewhere, while others were allowed to return to garrison in the Dutch Republic with their wives and families.[50] Some used their down time to invent new ways of killing. In 1626 Captain William Douglas offered the Dutch army a sophisticated firearm with a rate of fire equivalent to six musketeers, among other military innovations.[51] For many more, particularly the hundreds of sick and wounded, there was simply a need to rest, heal and recover.[52] The widows, of course, continued to petition the authorities and their kin for their pensions.

The conclusion of the Jacobean period of the Thirty Years' War ended without a major British field victory against the Habsburgs. It is doubtless because of this that there remains a lack of historical interest in the various levies and their engagements. The various deployments under Gray, Vere, Seton – or Mansfeld, highlight that King James was quite resolved to fight for the Palatinate either directly or by proxy via his Dutch allies and extant British regiments stationed in the Republic. Importantly, the events surrounding the Mansfeld levy led to a shift in policy by the British political elite. Angered at what was perceived to be the poor provisioning and support for the expeditionary forces, a group of Scottish nobles petitioned to be allowed to raise and equip their own army to fight on behalf of Elizabeth of Bohemia. The Scots wished to maintain 5,000 men for the recovery of the Palatinate, 'but they will have the paying and disposing of themselves'.[53] However, what had seemed to be a straightforward

48 Details of the manoeuvres of the English troops, and the composition of the companies are found in: British Library, Egerton Manuscript 2596, ff.163–165; TNA, SP84/127, ff.25–26 & ff147–151. With thanks to Simon Marsh for sharing his transcriptions of these sources. For Astley's (aka Ashley) rank and regiment see Ten Raa and De Bas, *Het Staatsche Leger*, III, p.181. For John Cromwell see also James Weylen, *The House of Cromwell*, edited and revised by John Gabriell Cromwell (London: Elliot Stock, 1897), p.15.

49 Boys, *London's News Press*, p.212.

50 Ferguson, *Scots Brigade*, I, pp.346–349.

51 Ferguson, *Scots Brigade*, I, pp.358–361. Douglas would go on to offer these weapons to the Swedish army with even greater claims for their firepower. His detailed description of his invention as offered to the Swedes can be found in SRA, Oxenstiernska samlingen, E588. Two letters of (Major) William Douglas to Axel Oxenstierna, undated, but the promotion indicates it was after his Dutch service as captain. In the second letter Douglas claims the Swedes owed him around 10,000 rixdaler (c. £2,500 sterling).

52 For the available medial provision see Steve Murdoch, '"Medic!" An Insight into Scottish Field Surgeons, Physicians and Medical Provision during the Thirty Years' War, 1618–1648', *Northern Studies*, vol. 48 (2017), pp.51–65.

53 Thomson (ed.), *The Chamberlain Letters*, pp.356–357. 19 January 1626.

policy under James – to side with Protestant allies to recapture the Palatinate for Elizabeth and Frederik V – descended into utter confusion under Charles I.

Direct war between England and Spain broke out in 1625 and rumbled on until 1630, though it was effectively over after the loss of 50 percent of the 15,000 soldiers and sailors who participated in the Cadiz expedition.[54] Charles also recklessly engaged in a needless war against his brother-in-law, Louis XIII of France, in 1627 ending with the humiliating Île de Ré campaign. An army of some 6,000 men equally composed of Scots, English and Irishmen were easily driven away by the French.[55] The French campaign was seen by Continental contemporaries as quite peripheral to the defence of the Stuart interests in the Palatinate. Christian IV of Denmark–Norway certainly believed his Stuart nephew had failed to support the Danish war against the Emperor by engaging in his Spanish and French campaigns.[56]

Despite frustration expressed by Christian IV, the engagement of British troops to Denmark represented one of the largest mobilisations of the war. It is well known that Charles promised some 6,000 Englishmen for Danish service under the command of the Welshman Sir Charles Morgan in 1627, of which it is generally held that fewer than 5,000 arrived.[57] Moreover, it represented the smaller of the British forces to come to the assistance of Denmark–Norway in this period. A staggering 13,700 Scots entered Danish service between 1627 and 1629 alone, albeit this total also contains a number of Irishmen and Ulster Scots.[58] Their most impressive achievement came at the siege of Stralsund in 1628, which saw three Highland regiments commanded by James Sinclair Baron Murckle, Alexander Lindsay Lord Spynie and Donald Mackay Lord Reay.[59] Hearing they were in difficulty, these troops were relieved by volunteer regiments of their countrymen drawn out of Swedish service. These 'Swedish-Scots' had been steadily recruited since 1624 in the hope of Sweden entering the war on the side of the Protestant powers. The Scots from the Swedish and Danish armies fell under the command of Sir Alexander Leslie, who also became governor of

54 John H. Elliot, 'Spain and the War' in Geoffrey Parker (ed.), *The Thirty Years' War* (2nd edition, London: Routledge, 2007), pp.68–69; Murdoch, *Britain*, p.66.

55 Murdoch, *Britain*, p.67; Boys, *London's News Press*, pp.151–152, 215–225.

56 Murdoch, *Britain*, pp.65–72.

57 E.A. Beller, 'The Military Expedition of Sir Charles Morgan to Germany, 1627–1629', *English Historical Review*, XLIII (1928), p.539; Murdoch, *Britain*, pp.203–204; Marks, 'Recognizing Friends from Foes', p.178. Marks puts the strength at 4,300 men. Victoria Yee has also done much to illuminate the role of Welsh soldiers other than Morgan among this contingent. See Victoria Yee 'An investigation into Welsh participation on the Protestant side of the Thirty Years' War', consulted online (10 December 2018) <https://jddavies.com/2016/09/12/an-investigation-into-welsh-involvement-in-the-protestant-side-of-the-thirty-years-war/>

58 Murdoch, *Britain*, p.206 and pp.202–225; Steve Murdoch, 'The Northern Flight: Irish Soldiers in Scandinavia' in O'Connor, Thomas and Lyons, Mary Ann (eds.), *The Ulster earls and baroque Europe: Refashioning Irish identities, 1600–1800* (Dublin: Four Courts Press, 2010), p.95.

59 Murdoch, *Britain*, pp. 215–217.

Stralsund in July 1628.[60] They inflicted the first serious defeat on the famous Imperial commander, Albrecht von Wallenstein, employing unconventional tactics, at least by Continental standards. As Robert Monro recorded in his regimental history, they marched in single column directly at their enemy. The musketeers expended all their ammunition and as the retired to the city 'to make their retreat good, [it] falls upon Captain Mac-Kenȝee with the old Scottish blades of our Regiment, to suppresse the enemies fury, they keeping face to their enemies, while their Camerades were retiring.'[61] An old-school Highland melee followed with devastating casualties on the Imperial side, compelling Wallenstein to lift the siege.[62] Over the next year and a half, Leslie led his troops in combined land and amphibious operations, clearing remnant Imperial garrisons with near impunity. This allowed for the 1630 landing of the massive Swedish army under Gustav II Adolf, who had taken on leadership of the Protestant cause after Christian IV concluded peace with the Emperor the previous year at the Treaty of Lübeck. The Danish campaign had been costly, however. As William Lithgow later penned in 1633:

Thus look to Denmark
where twelve thousand lye
Serving thine Uncle,
sharpest fortunes try[63]

These interventions in North Germany were not the only actions of the later 1620s, and both the Scots and English brigades in the Dutch Army participated at the siege of Groenlo (Grol, 1627) and 's-Hertogenbosch (Bois-le-Duc,1629).[64] An even larger army, commanded by James Marquess Hamilton, was conceived of in 1629 and landed in Germany in 1631 to support the Swedes. Warrants for 6,000 Scots and 6,000 English were issued. Among the colonels recruiting in England were Sir Jacob Astley, Sir James Ramsay 'the fair' and Sir James Hamilton, the latter two being Scots.[65] Elsewhere Captains John and Roger Powell recruited in Monmouth,

60 SRA, Germanica. Förhandlingar mellan Sverige och staden Stralsund. Gustav II Adolf's letter of appointment to Alexander Leslie, 21 July 1628.

61 Monro, *His Expedition*, vol. 1, p. 78.

62 These events are discussed in fuller detail in Murdoch and Grosjean, *Alexander Leslie*, pp.47–51.

63 William Lithgow, *Scotland's Welcome to her native sonne, and Sovereign Lord* (Edinburgh: J.W., 1633)

64 F.J.G. Ten Raa and F. De Bas, *Het Staatsche Leger 1568–1795: ondertoezicht van den Chef van den Generalen Staf, Deel IV, 1625–1648* (Breda: Nijhoff, 1918), pp.17–43; The actions of the English and Scots are recorded in Lincolnshire Archives: 8ANC8/29. Sir Edward Vere to unknown, 29 July / 8 August 1629; Ferguson, *Scots Brigade*, I, pp.310–311. Some soldiers had had enough of such actions. For example, Englishman George Cox (Joris Cocx) deserted in 1630 or 1631 leading to his name being nailed to the gallows of Leiden. Amsterdam Stadsarchief, Archief van de Notarissenter Standplaats Amsterdam. Attestatie, Jan Onderhoudt et al, 5 April 1633.

65 *Acts of the Privy Council of England, vol.46, 1630–1631*, edited by P.A. Penfold (London: HMSO, 1964), pp.376–378; Gloucester Borough Records, GBR/H/2/2 Order and letter book, 1631, pp. 167–170. I thank

Glamorgan and Carmarthen, while Sir Frederick Hamilton levied in Ireland.[66] Some 8,000 men under Hamilton landed in Germany where they joined some 12,000 Scots already in Swedish service.[67] In effect there were now two British armies operating alongside the Swedes. Hamilton insisted upon taking the coveted title of 'General of British' from his countryman, Sir James Spens of Wormiston.[68] The Swedes reacted to this by awarding Spens the title of 'General of Scots' to command the Scottish regiments which predated Hamilton's arrival.[69] It was these men who formed the famous Scots Brigade that fought with distinction at the Battle of Breitenfeld in 1631 while Hamilton's 'British' were deployed elsewhere. The request for Johan Banér to withdraw from Magdeburg because of heavy snow was met with a resolute affirmation that so long as he had one soldier standing beside him he would not give up because of the cold.[70] He remained resolutely in place, as did the Scots' reputation for being inured to the cold. Although Hamilton participated in some undeniably brave actions, his forces were riddled with disease, and some six reinforcement regiments, including Alexander Lord Forbes' Scots, Sir Frederick Hamilton's Irishmen and Sir Arthur Aston's English regiment, were consequently redirected Marquess directly into the Swedish army of Åke Tott rather than risk contagion.[71] Though Hamilton returned home the following year, he remained one of some 15 Scots to attain the rank of general within the Swedish army and he had proved a brave commander despite his largely ineffective army.[72] Moreover, many of those from across the British Isles who had enlisted with Hamilton remained in service.

While the actions of the Scottish commanders in the two British armies in Germany have been meticulously researched, the English among the cohort have received less attention from historians. This is surprising given how informed English readers were of their actions and campaigns through contemporary publications like *The Swedish Intelligencer* or *The Swedish Discipline*.[73] Adam Marks has done the most

Simon Marsh for sharing this source which confirms the identity of Astley and Ashley as one in the same.

66 For the Irish and Welsh see variously Murdoch, 'The Northern Flight', pp.97–101; Dominic Rooney, *The Life and Times of Sir Frederick Hamilton, 1590–1647* (Dublin: Four Courts Press, 2013), pp.51–76; Yee 'An investigation into Welsh participation'.

67 Alexia Grosjean, *An Unofficial Alliance: Scotland and Sweden, 1569–1654* (Leiden: Brill, 2003), pp.84–95. For Hamilton's 8,000 men Grosjean quotes Anon. [Friedrich Spanheim?], *Le SoldatSvedois* (Genève: Pierre Albert, 1633), p.50.

68 Grosjean, *An Unofficial Alliance*, p.89.

69 Murdoch and Grosjean, *Alexander Leslie*, p.54.

70 Murdoch and Grosjean, *Alexander Leslie*, p.58.

71 Grosjean, *An Unofficial Alliance*, pp.91–92.

72 Murdoch and Grosjean, *Alexander Leslie*, p.177.

73 The reception of the various volumes of William Watts, *The Swedish Intelligencer* (4 vols., London: Nath. Butter and Nicholas Bourne, 1632–1633) was recorded by the likes of John Rous. See Mary Ann Everett Green, (ed.), *Diary of John Rous, incumbent of Santon Downham, Suffolk* (London: Camden Society, 1856), p.75. For more on the reception of the *Swedish Discipline* see Boys, *London's News Press*, pp.143–148, 162–167, pp. 230–232; Anon., *The Swedish Discipline* (London: Nath. Butter, 1633).

comprehensive work on the regiment of Colonel George Fleetwood, following them from the formation of the regiment in Sweden in 1629 until its demise as an English unit in 1639.[74] Fleetwood was one of a number of English colonels to find their way into Swedish service, either through enlistment with Hamilton, or directly entering the Swedish army proper at an earlier date – men such as Colonels Thomas Conway and Thomas Muschamp, the latter having commanded native Swedish regiments since 1626.[75] Colonel Robert Monro in *His Expedition* records five English regiments in Swedish service in 1632: those of Colonels Arthur Aston, John Caswell (aka Cassells), George Fleetwood, James Ramsay and William Bellenden (the latter two being Scottish colonels of English regiments). However, he seems to have missed Sir Jacob Astley.[76] These men were not simply cannon fodder, but like the Scots, could also gain prestigious commands beyond commanding infantry regiments. For example, an astonishing number of 44 Scots (at least) were appointed governors of occupied cities and garrisons of the Holy Roman Empire between 1628 and 1648.[77] There was no bar to Englishmen being appointed to similar roles, albeit they were fewer in number. Most notable among the gubernatorial appointments and commandant positions included Colonel Thomas Muschamp (Marienwerder 1629), Major Thomas Grove (Buxtehude 1631), Colonel Arthur Aston (Osnabruck 1634, Nienburg 1636) and Colonel George Fleetwood (Griefswald 1638, Colberg 1641).[78] While numerous Englishmen had been governors of Dutch towns in the early phases of the Dutch Eighty Years' War, such positions were rarer by the 1640s.[79] Sir Charles Morgan's governorship of Bergen-op-Zoom in the years up to and including 1643 stands out (not least as Sir Thomas Morgan had been governor there in 1588).[80] Appointments, or the service of the English regiments, are often overlooked in favour of the actions of their commanders (or indeed junior officers) in the British Civil Wars that followed. In his 'Memoir of Sir Arthur Aston' the antiquarian George Steinman wrote off

74 Marks, 'England', pp.142–158.

75 F. Rudelius, *Kalmar RegementesPersonhistoria 1623–1927* (2 vols., Norrköping: AB Trycksaker, 1952), vol. 1, p.37.

76 Monro, *His Expedition*, The List of Officers in Chiefe, O2. Aston had been in Sweden since 1627 after being captured. He transferred his troops in 1629. See *Rikskansleren Axel Oxenstiernas Skrifteroch Brevvexling, Senareavdelining, Band I*, edited by Per Sondén (Stockholm: P.A. Norstedt, 1956), p.531.

77 Alexia Grosjean, 'A Century of Scottish Governorship in the Swedish Empire, 1574–1700', in Mackillop, Andrew and Steve Murdoch (eds.), *Military Governors and Imperial Frontiers, c.1600–1800* (Leiden: Brill, 2003), pp.60–70.

78 Their service in the these capacities can be found in Steve Murdoch and Grosjean, Alexia (eds.), *Scotland, Scandinavia and Northern European Biographical Database* [SSNE] consulted online at: <www.st-andrews.ac.uk/history/ssne>.

79 For early English governors see Markham, *The Fighting Veres*, pp.113, 123–124, 201–202, 211, 272, 348, 380–381. When the Dutch re-entered the war with Spain in 1621, Colonel John Ogle was city commandant of Utrecht. See Ten Raa and De Bas, *Het Staatsche Leger*, III, p.56.

80 Parliamentary Archives, HL/PO/JO/10/1/145. Certificate from Sir Charles Morgan, colonel of a regiment of foot [...] and Governor of Bergen-op-Zoom, 8 March 1643. For Sir Thomas see Markham, *The Fighting Veres*, pp.123–124.

Aston's service in the Swedish army in under a paragraph as simply being 'an hiatus of seven years' in his career.[81] Little has changed, as evidenced by Aston's biography on the *ODNB* in which this Swedish service is reduced to three meagre sentences.[82] Such contemptible disregard for the European archives leads to the failure to contextualise why some Thirty Years' War veterans could go on to command so efficiently during Wars of the Three Kingdoms (1639–1660).

The key example here is surely Alexander Leslie, who became Field Marshal of the quasi-independent Army of the Weser.[83] This *Armée Volante* was composed largely of the remnant Scottish regiments still in service by 1635, backed by German recruits and one regiment of Englishmen (Fleetwood's). When it looked briefly like the Swedes might come to a treaty with the Emperor, Leslie declared that he would keep his largely Scottish army in the field to secure the Palatinate for Elizabeth.[84] As it was the Swedes also remained engaged and what followed at Wittstock (1636) proved to be one of the most unlikely victories of the Thirty Years' War, with Leslie's army rescuing the Swedish army from certain defeat through some breathtaking battlefield deployments leading to a 360 degree encirclement of the enemy. By the end of the battle, Scottish generals not only commanded the centre battalia (Leslie), but also the left wing (James King) and the reserve (John Ruthven). Leslie managed to even shore up the right wing of Banér's retreating Swedes with five brigades, a fact attested to in Banér's official report just days after the battle.[85] Three years later, the Swede rewrote events to claim victory for himself and the Swedes alone.

Wittstock was not the only major action which saw Scottish regiments participate, or generals command in the field in 1636. At the battle of Saverne, Marechal John Hepburn died at the head of a large Scottish force in the French army.[86] If the death of Hepburn proved a serious setback to the French, there were further catastrophes awaiting the British on the Continent. The Battle of Kallo in June 1638 saw the worst defeat of the Dutch Army in the Eighty Years' War.[87] Reports variously discussed 2,000–4,000 Dutch soldiers killed and a further 2,000 captured, including some 600 Scots (most notably Colonels Balfour and Sandilands) and numerous English officers.

81 George Steinman, 'Memoir of Sir Arthur Aston', *The Gentleman's Magazine*, vol.155 (London: J.B. Nichols & Sons, 1834), p.145.

82 Basil Morgan, 'Aston, Sir Arthur', in *ODNB* accessed 5 June 2019. Adam Marks does better work. See Marks 'England', pp.36, 137, 141, 177.

83 Murdoch and Grosjean, *Alexander Leslie*, pp.75–85.

84 Murdoch and Grosjean, *Alexander Leslie*, p.75.

85 Steve Murdoch, Kathrin Zickermann, Kathrin and Adam Marks, 'The Battle of Wittstock 1636: Conflicting Reports on a Swedish Victory in Germany', *Northern Studies*, 43 (2012), pp.71–109.

86 Gustave Clanché, *Sir John Hepburn,Maréchal de France: inhumé à la Cathédrale de Toul en 1636* (Toul: Imprimerie Moderne, 1918), pp.11, 29, 30. Two dates are given for Hepburn's death. From the funerary monument (no longer extant), his death was recorded as 8 July, while later in the text, 21 July is the date given.

87 Ten Raa and De Bas, *Het Staatsche Leger*, IV, pp.101–114.

This led to intervention from Charles I to pay the ransom for their release.[88] More tragedy was to follow. William Lord Craven had raised a force of around 4,000 men to serve Elector Karl Ludwig, the eldest son of Elizabeth of Bohemia.[89] Lieutenant-General James King led 1,000 mostly British volunteers from Swedish service, including Colonel William Vavasour. Collectively they hoped to lend support to the small British–Palatine Army of Karl Ludwig, but they failed to prevent their defeat at Vlotho Bridge near Minden. Prince Rupert had impetuously charged before the army was properly deployed resulting in his own capture and that of Craven and Vavasour among others.[90] Fortunately Karl Ludwig himself managed to avoid capture. Craven remained in captivity until 1639 when he ransomed himself for £20,000 sterling and returned to London.[91] This was an interesting time for anyone to return to Britain.

It is sometimes stated that 1639 saw the end of meaningful Scottish participation in the European conflicts due to the outbreak of the Bishops' Wars (1639–1640). Surprisingly that proved not to be the case.[92] In 1638, Richelieu petitioned for 5,000 Scots to be raised and to join the existing *Regiment d'Hepburn* and the Irish regiment of Colonel Tyrell and these were guaranteed by Queen Henrietta Maria personally.[93] Not all of these arrived, but many thousands of Scots had remained on the Continent having prioritised the original aims of their service over the ongoing conflict at home. Many thousands of Thirty Years' War veterans formed the core of the Army of the Covenant raised to oppose Charles I in Scotland. Organised by Field Marshal Alexander Leslie, and with support from Sweden and France, a well-disciplined army humbled Charles I's forces twice during the Bishops' Wars.[94] Less well researched are the Scottish Royalist and English veterans who also came home to fight.[95] It is claimed that Sir Arthur Aston returned to England in 1639 with 'as many soldiers of note as he could bring', although how many awaits substantiation.[96]

88 Ferguson, *Scots Brigade*, I, pp.314, 322, 449–455. The ransom for some of the officers by Charles I is noted in J.A.Worp (ed.), *De Briefwisseling van Constantijn Huygens, Deel II, 1634–1639* (The Hague: Nijhoff, 1913), pp.382–383. Constantijn Huygens to Princess Amalia van Oranje, 25 July (regarding intervention for the English) and 10 August 1638 (for the release of four Scottish officers including Colonels Balfour and Sandilands). For the death toll see *ibid.*, xii; G. Dyfnallt Owen (ed.), *Report on the Manuscripts of the Right Honourable Viscount de Lisle. Vol. 6 Sydney Papers, 1626–1698* (London: HMSO, 1966), pp.146–147. Sir William Balantine to the Earl of Leicester, 2 July 1638.

89 Wilson, *Europe's Tragedy*, p.594; Murdoch and Grosjean, *Alexander Leslie*, p.90.

90 For Charles I's financial support of this army see Nadine Akkerman (ed.), *The Correspondence of Elisabeth Stuart, Queen of Bohemia, vol. II, 1632–1642* (Oxford: OUP, 2011), pp.670–677, 733, 751–4, 756–7.

91 R. Malcom Smuts, 'Craven, William, earl of Craven' in *ODNB*.

92 W.P. Guthrie, *The Later Thirty Years' War: From the Battle of Wittstock to the Treaty of Westphalia* (Westport, Connecticut: Greenwood Press, 2003), p. 257; Wilson, *Europe's Tragedy*, p. 594.

93 M. Avenel (ed.), *Lettres, Instructions Diplomatiques et Papiers d'état du cardinal de Richelieu* (8 vols., Paris: Impr. impériale, 1853–77), VI, pp.211–13. Cardinal Richelieu to M. de Bellièvre, 6 October and pp.238–240, Richelieu to M. de Bellièvre, 13 November 1638.

94 Murdoch and Grosjean, *Alexander Leslie*, pp.93–118.

95 An exception here is Marks, 'England', pp.163–188.

96 Steinman, *Memoir*, p.145.

Constantijn Huygens merely notes that many of the older English officers were on their way to England in 1640 in order to serve King Charles, but he does not name them other than Sir Thomas Culpeper. Rather, he pointed out that this presented an opportunity for Lord Craven to get the colonelcy of Culpeper's regiment.[97] More easily identified are the senior Royalists like Sir Patrick Ruthven who would go on to command an English garrison while besieged in Edinburgh Castle (1640) and lead the army in actions such as Edgehill (1642) and Cropredy Bridge (1644) as Lord General of the Royalist forces in England.[98] Contrary to the likes of Ruthven and Aston, whose return to Britain ended their participation in the Thirty Years' War, their Covenanter opponents only viewed their return as a temporary move until Charles I had re-evaluated his policies concerning Scotland. Indeed, as Alexia Grosjean has demonstrated, the Covenanters could only take their veterans home from Swedish service on the promise of reengaging in the European theatre once the troubles in Britain were resolved.[99] This was reinforced when Elector Karl Ludwig travelled with his uncle, Charles I, and sat beside him in the Scottish Parliament in 1641. So ensconced, the Elector was promised 10,000 men of the Scottish Army of the Covenant with which to reclaim his ancestral home in the Palatinate.[100] Only the outbreak of the Confederate Rebellion in Ireland prevented this and saw the Army of the Covenant being hastily redeployed to Ulster, dashing Karl Ludwig's hopes for gaining control of that veteran force. However, the intention here to continue in the war is evident and other Britons did continue in the wider anti-Habsburg campaigns.

It has similarly been suggested that the outbreak of the English Civil War in 1642 brought an abrupt end to meaningful English participation on the Continent.[101] Nevertheless, many doctrinaire Calvinists preferred Dutch service rather than participation in the inter-Protestant sectarian wars of Britain. Joining in civil conflicts that pitched contesting groups of Protestants against each other did not hold the same appeal for some as the defence of Protestantism against the Catholic threat posed by the Holy Roman Empire. As early as March 1642 some 30 fresh recruits were to be transported to Lieutenant-Colonel Ferdinando Knightley's company in the Dutch army at a time when all-out civil war in England was inevitable.[102] Indeed all four English regiments remained in the field under the command of Colonels William

97 J.A. Worp (ed.), *De Briefwisseling van Constantijn Huygens, Deel III, 1640–1644* (The Hague: Nijhoff, 1914), p.15. Constantijn Huygens to William Lord Craven, 21 March 1640.

98 Murdoch and Grosjean, *Alexander Leslie*, pp.113, 120–122.

99 Grosjean, *An Unofficial Alliance*, pp.169–170.

100 K.M. Brown et al. (eds.) *Records of the Parliament of* Scotland, Report of the committee to consider the business regarding the Prince Elector Palatinate approved, 12 November 1641 (<www.rps.ac.uk>); TNA, SP81/52, f.221. Scottish Parliament (Extract) 12 November 1641.

101 Trim, 'Calvinist Internationalism', p.1025.

102 Parliamentary Archives, HL/PO/JO/10/1/118. Draft order for Lieutenant Broomee to transport 30 recruits for Sir Ferdinando Knightley's Company, 21 March 1642.

Lord Craven, Baron George Goring, Sir Charles Morgan and Sir Henry Herbert.[103] The three regiments of the Scots–Dutch Brigade had also been brought back up to full strength and were now commanded by Colonels Sir Philip Balfour, Sir James Erskine and Sir John Kirkpatrick. Towards the end of 1642 Goring returned to England with a few Anglo-Dutch veterans and went on to have a well-documented career during the English Civil War. This caused the States of Holland to discuss suspending of payment for absentee English and Scottish officers and men.[104] However, Lieutenant-Colonel William Killigrew maintained Goring's regiment, and prepared them for the next big campaign under Frederick Henry, Prince of Orange. That is, those who were not indulging in petty crime. Two soldiers from Lieutenant-Colonel John Cromwell's company achieved a classic 'dine and dash', taking a meal in the Rotterdam inn, *De Vergulde Swaen*, before leaving for The Hague without paying.[105] However, the records of both the Rotterdam and Amsterdam legal archives suggest such behaviour was quite rare and discipline was maintained. It needed to be.

Elsewhere other Britons chose to serve in the French army rather than the Dutch. Some of these were Protestants simply keen to finish the war for the Palatinate in whichever army would take them. Others were Catholics and Episcopalians seeking to avoid persecution in Covenanted Scotland or elsewhere in 'Perfidious Albion'. The numbers of Scots active in French service by 1643 has been roughly estimated at 3,500 men, dispersed mostly between Lord James Douglas's *Régiment de Douglas* (ex-Hepburn's) and James Campbell Earl of Irvine's new *Garde Écossaise*. This contingent was to be built on with another three regiments and a total of 9,600 was expected to be reached by the end of the year.[106] They found themselves in action rather quickly: the *Garde Écossaise* participated in the Battle of Rocroi on 16 May 1643 while the other Franco-Scottish regiments were deployed elsewhere.[107] Sometimes these deployments were misconceived, with Douglas having to return from the Italian Peninsula as his

103 Ten Raa and De Bas, *Het Staatsche Leger*, IV, pp.241–243. Here the authors mistakenly call Sir Charles Morgan 'Thomas' and believe George Goring to be the later Earl of Norwich (his father), but it is otherwise an invaluable source. See also Ronald Hutton, 'Goring, George, Baron Goring' in *ODNB*; Edward M. Furgol, 'Morgan, Sir Charles' in *ODNB*. In Smuts, 'Craven, William, earl of Craven' in *ODNB*, Smuts omits Craven's service as a colonel of an English regiment throughout the 1640s, merely placing him at The Hague with Elizabeth of Bohemia.

104 Register van Holland en Westvriesland van de jaaren 1643–1644 (no place, no publisher, 1768–1772), p. 5. Resolution, 15 January 1643. Consulted online at: <https://books.google.nl/books?id=BGNJAAAAcAAJ&printsec=frontcover&dq=editions:IHf_BhkH_N8C&hl=nl&sa=X&ved=0ahUKEwjGtvvy09beAhXBLFAKHS7cAKE4PBDoAQg1MAI#v=onepage&q&f=false>

105 Stadsarchief Rotterdam, Notarissente Rotterdam (ONA) 306/217. Attestatie of verklaring, 18 February 1642.

106 William Bray (ed.), *The Diary of John Evelyn, volume IV* (London: Bickers and Son, 1882 edition), p. 382. Sir Richard Browne to Sir Edward Nicholas, 13–23 January 1642–43. G. Fotheringham (ed.), *The Diplomatic Correspondence of Jean de Montereul and the Brothers de Bellievre, French Ambassadors in England and Scotland, 1645–1648* (2 vols, Edinburgh: Scottish History Society, 1898–1899), II, p.337n; Stephane Thion, *French Armies of the Thirty Years' War* (Auzielle: L.R.T., 2008), pp.80, 82.

107 Thion, *French Armies of the Thirty Years' War*, pp.108, 129.

regiment simply could not function in the hot weather.[108] Now operating in Flanders, *Garde Écossaise* was topped up by new recruits. After the renewed civil war in Scotland in 1644, Royalist prisoners were sent to France where they fought against the Empire thereafter. The recruiting mechanisms for the English have not previously been extensively researched. Just before his death in 1643, Sir Charles Morgan had sent subordinates on a recruiting mission to England to bolster his regiment.[109] he implied success of that and other recruiting drives is implicit in the pay delivered by the States General to the company commanders for units noted as being at full strength later that year.[110] A perusal of the commissions issued by the Dutch army between 1642 and 1648 indicate no less than 65 new commissions being issued to some 60 Britons during the period of the English Civil War. Some of these were veterans and the commissions simply represent their promotions. However, many appear to be new officers arriving in service. These included such men as the young Sergeant Major Aubrey Vere, Earl of Oxford (commissioned on 7 November 1644).[111] He joined the regiment of Colonel Ferdinando Knightley, who had succeeded as colonel to Henry Herbert's regiment in October.[112] Just like with the Scottish commanders overseas, the English colonels in the Dutch Republic also coveted prisoners of war. In 1645 Colonel John Cromwell, Lieutenant-Colonel Ferdinando Knightley and Sergeant Major Thomas Hammond had requested permission to recruit as many prisoners as the English Parliament was prepared to send them. Goring's regiment was declined recruits due to the colonel serving Charles I. Rather the committee wanted to establish that the regiment really was firmly under Killigrew's command before allowing him troops.[113] By July permission was granted for Knightley to proceed with the levy.[114] So in an unexpected twist, it is now possible to confirm that many soldiers in the later Thirty Years' War were, in fact, veterans of the English Civil War.

108 Fotheringham (ed.), *The Diplomatic Correspondence of Jean de Montereul*, II, p.544. M. de Boisivon to M. de Brienne, 20 November 1643.

109 Parliamentary Archives HL/PO/JO/10/1/145. Certificate from Sir Charles Morgan, colonel of a regiment of foot [...] and Governor of Bergen-op-Zoom, 8 March 1643. Furgol, 'Morgan, Sir Charles' in *ODNB*.

110 Ferguson, *Scots Brigade*, I, p.328.

111 These numbers are extrapolated from a database of Dutch Military Commissions NT000914, 'Raad van State Commissieboeken' from the Nationaal Archief in the Hague. The index can be downloaded at: <https://www.nationaalarchief.nl/onderzoeken/index/nt00194?searchTerm=>; See also Victor Stater, 'Vere, Aubrey de, twentieth earl of Oxford' in *ODNB*. An interesting letter from the young earl was sent from Assenede in Flanders in September 1644 suggesting he was already with the English regiment occupying the town. See J.A. Worp (ed.), *De Briefwisseling van Constantijn Huygens, Deel IV, 1644–1649* (The Hague: Nijhoff, 1915), p.60. Constantijn Huygens to the Earl of Arundel, 2 September 1644.

112 Worp (ed.), *De Briefwisseling van Constantijn Huygens, Deel IV*, pp.91–92. Constantijn Huygens to Ferdinando Knightley, and another to Gravin von Löwenstein, both dated 19 October 1644. Huygens is expansive on Knightley gaining his colonelcy at Bergen-op-Zoom, not least as he felt this might aid in Knightley's wooing of the widowed 'Gravin von Löwenstein', though which one remains unclear.

113 TNA, SP21/8, f.198 (point 13). Proceedings of the Committee of Both Kingdoms, 16 April 1645; TNA, SP21/20, f.261. The Committee of Both Kingdoms to Mr Knightley, 23 May 1645.

114 TNA, SP21/21, f.67. The Committee of Both Kingdoms to Mr Knightley, 8 July 1645.

As the Dutch army under Prince Frederick Henry marched towards the River Lys in 1644, all seven British regiments had mobilised with him. In a brash move Colonel Erskine led his Scots across an incomplete bridge which the prince had ordered to be built across the Lys, overwhelming the defenders of the Spanish fortification on the other side with little resistance.[115] Some of the enemy were killed, and the rest were sent to the Prince as prisoners; more importantly, the action facilitated a swifter progress of the army than had been anticipated. Prince Frederick Henry pressed forward and fortified his encampments on the way. Both Henry Herbert's and William Lord Craven's regiments were frequently involved in ongoing small action against the Spanish, Craven losing some of his sappers in an action at Sas van Gent in mid August.[116] By the end of the campaigning season the Scots were occupying Selsaten while the English were based around Assenede.[117] They spent the winter and spring recuperating. Two English officers – Captain Joseph Brown and Ensign Nicholas Cave (of Knightley's regiment) – had to provide an affidavit at the request of a Dutch innkeeper to the effect that, although being at his inn in the afternoon, they were unaware of any untoward noise.[118] We can draw our own conclusions, but perhaps they had reason to enjoy a lively pint as a big military push was coming. There were others who were simply not game for campaigning and had other things on their mind. Another English soldier, William Barck, deserted his regiment in 1645 to elope and live in sin with Janettje Makeroel, the widow of a fellow soldier. This caused consternation to the Dutch neighbours who reported him.[119] But perhaps the high jinks and low morals are unsurprising. All four English regiments were being mustered after the winter season and joined the three Scots units to march with Frederick Henry deeper into Flanders.[120]

The main actions took place in late autumn. Lieutenant-Colonel William Killigrew (commanding Goring's regiment) was applauded for the taking of the fort of Kieldrecht on 11 October.[121] Two weeks later Colonel John Kirkpatrick's actions in hastening the capture of the city were applauded by contemporaries.[122] Reports circulating in England suggested that on the march towards Hulst, Craven and Cromwell had fallen out over the ordering of the troops. Sir Robert Honeywood reported (from London)

115 Ferguson (ed.), *Scots Brigade*, I, pp. 315–16.

116 Worp (ed.), *De Briefwisseling van Constantijn Huygens*, IV, pp.34–36. Constantijn Huygens to Princess Amalia van Oranje, 11 & 12 August 1644.

117 Ferguson (ed.), *Scots Brigade*, I, p.316.

118 Stadsarchief Rotterdam, Notarissente Rotterdam (ONA) 344/196. Attestatie of verklaring, 3 April 1645.

119 Stadsarchief Rotterdam, Notarissente Rotterdam (ONA) 333/133. Attestatie of verklaring, 2 May 1645.

120 Frederick Henry (Prince of Orange), *Memoires de Frederic Henry Prince D'Orange* (Amsterdam: Pierre Humbert, 1733), p.331 & 334. Regiments are named by colonel, thus Goring is presented rather than Killigrew. An English summary of this mobilisation is given in Ferguson, *Scots Brigade*, I, pp.315–316, 324.

121 Worp (ed.), *De Briefwisseling van Constantijn Huygens*, IV, p.228. Constantijn Huygens to Princess Amalia van Oranje, 12 October 1645.

122 Worp (ed.), *De Briefwisseling van Constantijn Huygens*, IV, p.237. Constantijn Huygens to Princess Amalia van Oranje, 24 October 1645.

that the two colonels removed themselves from camp and fought a duel on horseback resulting in Craven killing Cromwell, and then fleeing for France.[123] This was untrue. The presence of Craven in the army was explicitly mentioned in dispatches weeks later while Dutch sources appear silent on the matter. Moreover John Cromwell met with his cousin, Oliver Cromwell, several times in the following years.[124] With Cromwell very much alive he, along with all seven British regiments, took part in the Siege of Hulst.[125] Here the British contributed 64 out of 285 companies in the Prince of Orange's army – or not far off a quarter of his fighting strength.[126] Of these, the Scots contributed 24 companies and the English a staggering 40 (over 3,000 men). The British regiments were stationed together on the right-hand side of the army, repeatedly assaulting the positions facing them until the surrender of the city on 4 November. This proved to be the final major operation by the Dutch in the Thirty Years' War.

With the war between Spain and the Dutch Republic effectively over, there were changes to the command structure. Aubrey de Vere, the Earl of Oxford, had disgraced himself by killing a man 'in self-defence', but was apparently forgiven by the Prince of Orange due to his remorsefulness. He also had allies among the Dutch elite, with Constantijn Huygens, his cousin, also seeking the intervention of Elisabeth, Countess of Löwenstein, to enable the completion of his rehabilitation and help restart his military career.[127] Such intervention clearly worked and he was promoted full colonel on 8 December within weeks of Huygens' letter.[128] A few months later, William Killigrew finally earned the colonelcy of Goring's regiment after the latter sold his commission for £2,000 and retired to Brussels to join his father.[129] However, there was little for the British colonels to do other than remain in garrison until the conclusion of the Spanish war in 1648. Rumours that this might lead to the return of the Anglo-Dutch brigade to join the Royalist cause were soon rubbished. One pamphlet even

123 TNA, SP 16/511, ff.11–13. Robert Honeywood to Henry Vane, 7 October 1645.

124 For Craven see Worp (ed.), *De Briefwisseling van Constantijn Huygens*, IV, p.240. Constantijn Huygens to Princess Amalia van Oranje, 27 October 1645. For Cromwell see James Heath, *Flagellum, or, The life and death, birth and burial of Oliver Cromwell faithfully described in an exact account of his policies and successes, not heretofore published or discovered* (London: S.T., 1663), pp.40–50.

125 Frederick Henry, *Memoires*, pp.351–359; Ten Raa and De Bas, *Het Staatsche Leger*, IV, pp.143–149; Olaf van Nimwegen, *The Dutch Army and the Military Revolutions, 1588–1688* (Woodbridge: The Boydell Press, 2010), pp.276–278.

126 The companies of the army are listed in Rijksmuseum, 'Beleg van Hulst door Frederik Hendrick, 1645' by Claes Jansz. Visscher (1645). See also Rijksmuseum, 'Beleg van Hulst, 1645' by Abraham Diriksz. Santvoort (1645) and the same artist's updated 'BelegenVerouvering van Hulst door Frederik Hendrik' (1646). Each shows the Scots and English brigaded together though one orientates the scene differently. For the latter see Rijksmuseum, Anon., 'Obsidio Huls, tenae civitatis et fortality'(1645).

127 Worp (ed.), *De Briefwisseling van Constantijn Huygens*, IV, p.365. Constantijn Huygens to Elizabeth, Gravin van Löwenstein, undated, but *c.*November 1646.

128 Nationaal Archief, The Hague. NT000914, 'Raad van State Commissieboeken', 8 December 1646.

129 TNA, SP16/515/1, f.46. Sir John Conyers to Edward Viscount Conway, 6/18 March 1647.

recorded William Lord Craven in front of his assembled men declaring that he would lead them against any enemy 'to the true faith of Christianity' (i.e. Protestantism), but emphatically stating that he would not take them into England.[130] Colonel John Cromwell did return to England, but apparently as a messenger from the Prince of Wales seeking to intercede with his cousin Oliver to spare the life of King Charles.[131]

Although the Dutch had effectively been out of the fighting since 1646, there were other British units in action elsewhere. Again, the Scottish aspect of this has been looked at in some detail.[132] Decommissioned soldiers of the Army of the Solemn League joined the Swedes in Germany in 1647 in time for the final push towards Prague the following year. It had been Alexander Leslie's intention to send out a full 10,000 men to Sweden to help finish the war once he reduced his army on their return from England in January 1647. This had been organised through the mediation of his long-time friend (and opponent from Marston Moor), James King Lord Eythin the previous year. Leslie's rational was twofold. Firstly, he wished to keep the soldiers of his vaunted 'Army of the Solemn League and Covenant' out of the hands of the increasingly fractious fanatics running both Scotland and England (as he viewed them). Secondly, he still believed the war for the Palatinate to be unfinished business.[133] However, Marquess Hamilton's gaining control of the Scottish Parliament scuppered the full levy and only two regiments have been shown to have reached Swedish service. They joined the remaining Scots in the French army. The *Garde Écossaise* and James Douglas's *Régiment de Douglas* (formerly Hepburn's) distinguished themselves repeatedly, most notably at the Battle of Lens in 1648.[134] This proved to be the last pitched battle of the Thirty Years' War and one in which the Scots remained the last infantry regiment on the field before they were finally relieved by French cavalry units. However, there were still ongoing campaigns including the Swedish assault on Prague. In this eleventh-hour action we find the last known Scottish (or British) casualty killed in action in the course of the conflict uncovered so far. His name was Major Alexander Kinnemond, and he died during an assault on Prague's fortifications on 20 October 1648, just four days before the signing of the Treaty of Westphalia that ended the Thirty Years' War.[135] It is worth noting that at the time of that assault, 10 out of the 21 native Swedish infantry regiments had Scottish colonels, while George Fleetwood still at the head of a regiment (albeit no longer an English one).[136] Eight

130 Anon. [S.G.], *The Resolution of His Highness, the Prince of Wales concerning his coming into England to assist His Royal Father, the King* (London: N.P., 1648), pp.5–6. 'A declaration of the Prince of Wales and the proceeding of the Lord Craven, touching the King's Majesty' by William Vandere, Delft, 2 July 1648.

131 Heath, *Flagellum*, pp.67–69; Weylen, *The House of Cromwell*, p.15.

132 Murdoch and Grosjean, *Alexander Leslie*, chapter 7.

133 Murdoch and Grosjean, *Alexander Leslie*, p.165.

134 Guthrie, *The Later Thirty Years' War*, p.192.

135 Murdoch and Grosjean, *Alexander Leslie*, p.166.

136 For Fleetwood's regiment see variously Krigsarkivet Stockholm, KrA/0022/1642/14 (1642) through until KrA/0022/1648/20 (1648).These show Fleetwood's regiment in continuous service around Colberg

more German regiments were also commanded by Scots. In the cavalry, Robert Douglas served as a newly promoted lieutenant-general joining Alexander 'Arvid' Forbes among the senior Swedish staff officers at the conclusion of the war.[137]

The role of such commanders – and of course the central position of Elizabeth of Bohemia – points to the British being more engaged in the war than is typically understood. Indeed, assumptions about when British interest in either Elizabeth or the wider Protestant cause outside Britain ceased are clearly shown here to be fallacious. The 1639 or 1642 end dates are a figment of the imagination resulting from a myopic focus on the British Civil Wars. Many Britons were far more concerned with the ongoing defence of Protestantism (as discussed above): for others, the veterans of the British Civil Wars, service overseas was preferable to imprisonment, execution or an intolerable life under a regime they despised.

Recent scholarship has, to some degree addressed these fallacies by highlighting the role of the senior commanders and the actions they engaged in. Moreover,by looking to the corpus of letters like those of the Scottish soldier, Drummer James Spens (in Dutch, Swedish and then Dutch VOC service), we now have a greater understanding of many equally important aspects of the war. This includes the role of the common solder and their motivations for participation in the war, and in Spens' case, for leaving it for the East Indies just as Gustav II Adolf was at the height of his victories in Europe.[138] The English soldier Robert Philips also had personal reasons to choose his theatre: he remained in the Dutch Republic rather than participate in the British Civil Wars and we can speculate as to why. In March 1640 he and his English wife, Anneken French, christened their newborn child in the Dutch Reformed Church in Bergen-op-Zoom.[139] He had a young family a settled life in the community, and secure employment in the Anglo-Dutch Brigade. Through scrutiny of Continental sources, we are moving beyond simply the great men and big battles in which the British participated. The role of women, widows, children and orphans in the war is now finally being properly researched.[140] To many people it is these, non-combatant aspects that can engage the historical imagination as much as the war itself. And on those subjects, there is still much work to be done.

where Fleetwood was also governor.

137 Murdoch and Grosjean, *Alexander Leslie,* pp.167–168.

138 Steve Murdoch, Alexia Grosjean and Siobhan Talbott. 'Drummer Major James Spens: Letters from a Common Soldier Abroad, 1617–1632' in *Northern Studies*, 47 (2015), pp.76–101

139 See Zeeuwsarchief, DTBL Terneuzen 1A (ondertrouwregister 1631–1796), f.15. Baptismal record, 10 March 1640. Consulted online at <www.zeeuwsarchief.nl>. Philips was married to the English woman 'Anneken' French and was a soldier under Sir Charles Morgan in Captain Huntly's company.

140 Siobhan Talbott, 'Scottish Women and the Scandinavian Wars of the Seventeenth Century', *Northern Studies* 40 (2007), pp.102–127; Murdoch and Zickermann, 'Bereft of all human help?', pp.114–134. The SSNE database contains information several hundred soldiers' wives, sisters and daughters from this period.

1

Gerat Barry: Soldier, Military Theorist and the Irish Rebellion of 1641

Keith Dowen

Introduction

Of the numerous veterans of the Continental wars of the early 17th century who also served in the Wars of the Three Kingdoms, Gerat Barry is seldom remembered. Condemned to posterity as 'old and unfortunate' by the Earl of Castlehaven for his failures in Ireland, Barry received little praise from his fellow countrymen.[1] As one detractor commented, 'for a politician I cannot esteem him one especially when I behold him in his outward appearance, which renders him very homely and despicable.'[2] Sadly, these opinions have been so influential, that his earlier distinguished career on the Continent has been largely overlooked.[3] Having served for many years in the Spanish army, it was during this period of his life that Barry took advantage of his many years of practical experience as a soldier to pen a treatise on military discipline. Of course, this did not make Barry unique. Other soldiers turned writers included fellow Low Countries veterans Edward Davies (*The Art of War and England's Traynings*, 1619), Henry Hexham (*The Principles of the Art Militarie 1637–1640*) and Robert Ward (*Anima'dversions of Warre*, 1639). Instead the importance of Barry's work was that it not only reflected Spanish–Habsburg rather than Dutch military practice (as most of other English-language treatises did), but that it was the earliest military book of note by an Irishman.[4]

1 James Touchet, *The Memoirs of James Lord Audley, Earl of Castlehaven* (London, 1680), p.30.

2 Quoted in Kenneth Wiggins, *Anatomy of a siege. King John's Castle. Limerick, 1642* (Woodbridge: Boydell, 2001), p.57.

3 An exception to this is Eduardo de Mesa, 'Gerat Barry: swordsman, military theorist, entrepreneur and servitor of the Spanish Monarchy', in *The Irish Sword*, Vol. XXX no. 120 (2015), pp.151–156.

4 De Mesa, 'Gerat Barry', pp.151–156; Harman Murtagh, 'Irish Soldiers Abroad', in I. Bartlett and K. Jeffrey (eds.), *A Military History of Ireland* (Cambridge: Cambridge University Press, 1996), p.295; and David R. Lawrence, *The Complete Soldier. Military Culture in Early Stuart England, 1603–1645* (Leiden: Brill, 2009), p.213. In May 1626 the total number of British soldiers serving in the State's army was estimated at 19,000 foot and total number of British soldiers serving in the State's army was estimated at 19,000 foot and 600 horse. See Hugh Dunthorne, *Britain and the Dutch Revolt 1560–1700* (Cambridge: Cambridge University Press, 2013).

Service in Flanders

As was the case with many of his fellow countrymen, Gerat Barry gained the majority of his military experience serving with the Spanish Army of Flanders in the Low Countries during the Eighty Years' War (1568–1648). Apart from the significant numbers of Irishmen who had migrated to Spain and Portugal after the failed Desmond Rebellion of 1583, the first Irish units to enter Spanish service were those of Sir William Stanley's regiment which had notoriously defected from the English army at Deventer in 1587.[5] Following a mutiny against their predominantly English officers, the Irish nonetheless remained in Spanish service albeit as independent companies.[6] With the Hiberno-Spanish defeat at Kinsale in 1601/2 and the ending of the Nine Years' War a year later, further Irish soldiers and their families began arriving in the Spanish realms in the Spanish realms in large numbers.[7] Numbered among them was Gerat Barry who, along with many other Irishmen and their families, had been allowed to leave Ireland under the terms of surrender negotiated by the Spanish commander Juan de Águila.[8] Initially serving as a marine in the Atlantic Fleet in the Irish company of Hugh Mostyn, the 'Armada del mar Océano' had officially been established in 1580s to patrol the eastern end of the transatlantic trade routes.[9] According to Admiral Don Diego Brochero in 1597, Irish volunteers were particularly sought after as they were 'a people who tolerate hard work and are not killed off as easily as the Spanish by bad food or the cold; because their land is much colder than this, they go around almost naked, sleep on the ground and live off oats,

5 Eduardo De Mesa, *The Irish in the Spanish Armies in the Seventeenth Century* (Woodbridge: Boydell, 2014), p.13; Albert J. Loomie, *The Spanish Elizabethans: The English Exiles at the Court of Philip II* (New York: Fordham University Press, 1963), pp.138–139; Thomas Heywood, *Cardinal Allen's Defence of Sir William Stanley's Surrender of Deventer* (The Chetham Society: Manchester, 1851), pp.xxii–xxxii; and Murtagh, 'Irish Soldiers', p. 295.

6 Ciarán Óg O'Reilly, 'The Irish Mercenary Tradition in the 1600s', in J. France (ed.), *Mercenaries and Paid Men. The Mercenary Tradition in the Middle Ages* (Leiden: Brill, 2008), pp.383–395 at p.384; and Roger B. Manning, *Apprenticeship in Arms. The Origins of the British Army 1585–1702* (Oxford: Oxford University Press, 2004), p.86.

7 O'Reilly, 'The Irish Mercenary Tradition', p.384 and Eduardo De Mesa, 'The Irish "nation" and the Councils of State and War, 1603–1644', in. O.R. Morales (ed.), *Redes de nación y espacios de poder. La comunidad irlandesa en España y la América Española 1600–1825* (Madrid: Albatros Ediciones, 2012), pp.155–170, at p.156. See also Ciaran O'Scea, 'From Munster to La Coruña Across the Celtic Sea: Emigration, Assimilation, and Acculturation in the Kingdom of Galicia (1601–1640)', in *Obradoiro de Historia Moderna*, no. 19 (2010), pp.9–38, at p.18.

8 Padraig Lenihan, 'Barry, Gerat', in H.C.G. Matthew and B. Harrison (eds.), *Oxford Dictionary of National Biography, vol. 4, Barney–Bellasis* (Oxford: Oxford University Press, 2004), p.130; O'Scea, 'From Munster to La Coruña', p.17; *Pacta Hibernia; or, A History of the Wars in Ireland* (Dublin: The Hibernia Press Company, 1810), pp.425–26, and see De Mesa, 'Gerat Barry', pp.151–152.

9 Gerat Barry, *A Discourse of Military Discipline* (Brussels, 1634) and George Modelski and William R. Thompson, *Seapower in Global Politics 1494–1993* (London: Macmillan Press, 1988), pp.268–270. The company of marines had been established in 1603.

meat and water without drinking wine.'[10] In June 1605 Barry's company, as part of the marine tercio under *Maestre de Campo* Pedro Sarmiento, was transferred to Flanders to reinforce Ambrogio Spínola's offensive against the Dutch. Engaged en route by a superior Dutch fleet off Dover, Barry was injured in the arm by a cannonball whilst commanding 40 men in the prow of one of the Spanish galleons.[11]

Having arrived in Dunkirk in December, Mostyn's company was attached to the Tercio of *Maestre de Campo* Henry O'Neill (also known as the 'Tercio Viejo Irlandés' and after 1616 the 'Tercio Irlandés del Conde de Tyrone'), which had recently been constituted out of the various groups and independent companies of Irishmen in Flanders.[12] The following year, Barry fought at the siege of Rheinberg where his personal bravery was later rewarded with a special grant (*ventaja particular*) of four escudos per month in addition to his regular pay.[13] After many years of service he was promoted to the position of *alférez* or ensign (also the second in command of a company) in 1623 and also made *ayudante* (adjutant) to the sergeant major in Tyrone's Tercio.[14] The following year, commissioned captain of a company by Infanta Isabel Clara Eugenia, Barry was among the many thousands of men besieging the Dutch city of Breda.

Located on the road to Antwerp near the border of the Dutch Republic and Spanish Flanders, the city was of vital strategic importance to both sides. Lasting nearly 10 months and costing thousands of lives it was observed that the siege served as 'a seminary, as it were, of military discipline'.[15] Clearly affected by his experiences, in 1627 Barry ventured into writing for the first time, publishing *The Siege of Breda*, in which he 'set forth in the Inglish tongue' the events of one of the most celebrated Spanish victories of the Dutch wars.[16] However, far from being an original account, it was little more than a translation of Hermannus Hugo's 1626 *Obsidio Bredana* into which he inserted a number of additional pages extolling the role the Irish played in the siege. Likewise, no mention was made of the fact that an 'official' translation of

10 Quoted in David Goodman, *Spanish Naval Power 1589–1665. Reconstruction and defeat* (Cambridge: Cambridge University Press, 2002), p.207.

11 De Mesa, 'Gerat Barry' p.152; Antonio J.R. Hernández, *Los Tercios de Flandes* (Madrid: Nowtilus, 2015), pp.254–255; Peter Limm, *The Dutch Revolt 1568–1648* (London: Routledge, 1989), p.66.

12 Murtagh, 'Irish Soldiers Abroad' p.295; De Mesa, 'The Irish in the Spanish Armies' pp.13–14; Jerrold Casway, 'Henry O'Neill and the formation of the Irish regiment in the Netherlands, 1605', in *Irish Historical Studies* Vol. 18 No. 72 (1973), pp.481–488; Michelin Walsh, 'O Neills in Exile', *Seanchas Ardmhacha: Journal of the Armagh Diocesan Historical Society* Vol. 8. No. 1 (1976), pp.55–68 p.58; O'Reilly, 'The Irish Mercenary Tradition' pp.384–385, and Henry Gráinne, *The Irish Military Community in Spanish Flanders 1586–1621* (Irish Academic Press, 1992), pp.44 and 63. Tercios were formed of 10 or 12 companies of varying sizes. Although each company ideally consisted of around 250 men, in practice this could vary from between 100 to 150 men.

13 Brendan Jennings, *Wild Geese in Spanish Flanders* (Dublin: Irish Manuscripts Commission, 1964) pp.102–103 and De Mesa, 'Gerat Barry', p.152.

14 Jennings *Wild Geese* p. 190 and De Mesa, 'Gerat Barry', p. 152.

15 Henry Gage, *The siege of Breda written in Latin by the R.F. Herman Hugo* (Ghent, 1627), p.6. A less accomplished translation may be found in Barry, 1627, p.6. See also Herman Hugo, *Obsidio Bredana* (Antwerp, 1626), p.5.

16 Gerat Barry, *The Siege of Breda by the Armes of Phillip the Fourt* (Louvain, 1627).

1.1 A plan of the 1624 Siege of Breda. The Irish positions can be seen in the top right. (Image courtesy of the Rijksmuseum Amsterdam. Object Number RP-P-OB-81.085)

Hugo's Latin text had already been published by Colonel Sir Henry Gage, an English officer in Spanish service.[17] Instead, the purpose for Barry's work appears to have been as much political as educational. Evidence of this is to be found in the book's dedication which explicitly states he intended the work to 'enlighten my beloveded contrymen with the honor of thy Heroicall Acts' fighting under the 'invincible Champion of the Catholique Church' Ambrogio Spínola. In other words, a united 'Irish nation' fighting alongside the armies of the Counter Reformation.[18]

A year after *The Siege of Breda* was published, Barry was placed in command of a company in Tyrone's Tercio and was subsequently sent to garrison Ostend in 1631.[19] That same year, as part of the attempt to occupy the islands of Goeree and Overflakee, Barry fought in the battle of the Slaak on 12 and 13 September where a Dutch fleet under Vice-Admiral Marinus Hollaer inflicted a defeat on the Spanish ships in a daring night engagement.[20] Having fought at the siege of Speyer, where his conduct was again highly praised, in October 1632 a number of companies, including Barry's, were disbanded due to low numbers. In December he was garrisoned at Sas van Gent and in addition to being granted 40 crowns per month was awarded the largely honorific title of 'Counsellor of War of Flanders' in recognition of his long service.[21]

'A Discourse of Military Discipline'

In 1634, having gained 33 years military experience 'in this my presente profession of armes, in his Catholike Majesties service' Barry penned an analytical treatise entitled *A Discourse of Military Discipline.*[22] Dedicated to David Barry, 1st Earl of Barrymore, whom Barry claims was a kinsman, the treatise was written 'to inlighten my beloved countrymen. Such as are not skillful in warres, and are desirouse to inter into the noble profession of Armes'.[23] As the first member of the family to embrace Protestantism, the dedication of the book to the Earl of Barrymore may at initially seem at odds with Gerat Barry's apparent 'militant' Catholicism. However, like Barry, Barrymore was from an 'Old English' family (the descendants of medieval settlers who nearly all adhered to the Catholic faith). It is therefore possible that Barry's dedication to him was as a reminder of where he felt his kinsman's loyalties should lie.

17 Deana M. Rankin, 'The Art of War: Military Writing in Ireland in the Mid Seventeenth Century' (unpublished PhD Thesis, University of Oxford, 1999) p.51; and Dunthorne, *Britain and the Dutch Revolt 1560*–1700, pp.24–25. Henry Gage had joined the Spanish Army of Flanders in 1620 following the expiration of the truce with the Dutch Republic and enjoyed a successful career. He served the Royalist cause during the Civil Wars becoming governor of Oxford. He died in 1645 after receiving a mortal wound at Abingdon.

18 Rankin, 1999, pp.52–54, and Barry, 1627.

19 De Mesa, *The Irish in the Spanish Armies*, pp.21 and 75–79 and Jennings, *Wild Geese*, p.253.

20 De Mesa, 'Gerat Barry', p. 154, and Adri P. van Vliet, 'Foundation, Organization and Effects of the Dutch Navy (1568–1648)' in M. van der Hoeven (ed.), *Exercise of Arms: Warfare in the Netherlands, 1568–1648* (Leiden: Brill, 1997), pp. 153–172, at p.167.

21 Jennings, *Wild Geese*, p.263, and De Mesa, 'Gerat Barry', p.154.

22 Barry, *A discourse of military discipline.*

23 Barry, *A discourse of military discipline.*

1.2 The title page of *A Discourse of Military Discipline* by Gerat Barry, 1634. (Royal Collection Trust/©Her Majesty Queen Elizabeth II 2019)

Although dismissed by Maurice Cockle in his 1900 publication *A Bibliography of Military Books up to 1642* as 'a compilation of no great merit', Barry's work sheds valuable light on Spanish military tactics and in so doing dismisses many modern assumptions regarding the capabilities of the Army of Flanders.[24] Designed to be studied by captains and sergeants, the men primarily responsible for training and discipline, as an analytical treatise the *Discourse* addressed a number of subjects encompassing the duties of officers and soldiers, battlefield tactics, fortifications and even the various types of gunpowder weapons used in siege warfare (known as 'fireworks').[25] Although Barry's treatment of 'firewourkes' was later disparaged by one anonymous author, his *Discourse* nonetheless demonstrated an appreciable knowledge of siegecraft undoubtedly obtained at Breda and other similar engagements.[26] Indeed, with sieges dominating warfare in the Low Countries, it was increasingly expected that soldiers should at least understand the rudiments of siege warfare.[27]

Acutely aware of the failures of the current Spanish officer class, and following in the footsteps of the 'perfect officer' genre of military literature, Barry's *Discourse* stressed the need for men to be promoted solely on the basis of merit and proven

24 Maurice Cockle, *A Bibliography of Military Books up to 1642* (London: The Holland Press, 1959), pp.101–102.

25 Lawrence, *The Complete Soldier*, p.195.

26 Geoffrey Parker, *The Army of Flanders and the Spanish Road 1567–1659* (Cambridge, Cambridge University Press, 2004), pp.4–9; H.L. Zwitzer, 'The Eighty Years War' in M. Van de Hoeven (ed.), *Exercise of Arms*, pp.33–57 and pp.41–42; Charles Oman, *A History of the Art of War in the Sixteenth Century* (London: Meuthen & Co, 1937), pp.541–545 and Herbert Gillman (ed.), 'The Rise and Progress of the Rebellion in Munster, 1642', in *Journal of the Cork Historical and Archaeological Society*, Volume II (1896), pp.63–70, at p.70. '*He is now retired to his privacy and desires us all to leave him – and so I – to the framing of his 'laderiscoes', grandoes, fireworks, altissimoes, batriscoes, tormentabilities, faculations, trepidations, penetrandulas' and all other strategems, the meaning whereof I omit for the want of the words of art*'.

27 Lawrence, *The Complete Soldier*, pp.350–352.

abilities rather than favouritism or social standing.[28] Indeed, the promotion of inexperienced 'grandees' to positions of command by the Spanish Council of State had become such a serious issue by the 1630s that it threatened the discipline and moral of the army.[29] As Don Carlos Coloma Marquis of Espinar had observed, evidently with some frustration, men 'wanted to start out as generals and soldiers on the same day'.[30]

As an experienced soldier, Barry fully appreciated the necessity of regular training, believing that 'no man can reduce into perfection those thinges wherof he is ingnorante, and knoweth not the arte, withoute much practice, and specially in this soe noble and couriouse arte, who for the executiones therof, with prudence and auctoritie is required both longe and diligent practice and theorike'.[31] Mindful of this, the *Discourse* emphasises the need for good thorough education which not only included the practicalities of handling a variety of weapons, but also encompassed history and mathematics.[32] This opinion was also shared by English veteran Robert Barret, who noted in 1598 that an officer should be 'very skilfull in Arithmetike, for without the same, he could hardly perform his office.'[33] This need becomes immediately apparent when reading the section 'Treatinge of severall sortes of Squadrones' which explained the process of organising various formations in the field. It reveals that contrary to the common assumption, by the 1630s the Spanish tercios were highly flexible units able to rapidly adapt to changing battlefield situations.[34] Indeed, the view that Spanish military tactics were at best conservative, or at worst backwards compared to the 'revolutionary' methods employed by the Dutch, is largely false.[35] Whilst it is true that the Spanish remained unconvinced by the Dutch model, this was largely based the proven track record of their armies.[36] After all, the rarity of pitched battles in the Low Countries meant that the reforms instituted by Prince Maurice of Orange and his cousins William Louis and John of Nassau, saw little practical application. Even at Nieuwpoort in 1600 the Dutch victory had been far from assured.[37] Nonetheless, this did not mean that Spanish military theory stagnated or that there was little interest in military science. It is thus perhaps somewhat surprising to know that in the years following the publication of Francisco de Valdés' *Espejo y Disciplina Militar* in 1586, the Spanish produced military

28 Barry, *A discourse*, pp.20–21.

29 Parker, *The Army of Flanders*, pp.102–103, and Fernando G. de Leon, *The Road to Rocroi. Class, Culture and Command in the Spanish Army of Flanders, 1567–1659* (Leiden: Brill, 2009), pp. 183, 185–188 and 200.

30 Quoted in Parker, *The Army of Flanders* p.102.

31 Barry, *A discourse*, pp.10, 162–163.

32 Barry, *A discourse*. See for example pp.9, 44 and 133.

33 Robert Barret, *The Theorike and Practike of Moderne Warres* (London, 1598), p.94. The similarity of some passages between Barret and Barry suggests the latter was familiar with Barret's work.

34 De Mesa, *The Irish in the Spanish Armies*, pp.10–11.

35 De Mesa, *The Irish in the Spanish Armies*, p.10.

36 Keith Roberts, *Pike and Shot Tactics 1590–1660* (Oxford: Osprey, 2010), pp.26 and 45; Keith Roberts (ed.), *Barriffe: A Civil War Drill Book* (Leigh-on-Sea: Partizan Press, 1988), unpaginated.

37 Jan Piet Puype, 'Victory at Nieuwpoort, 2 July 1600', in M. Van der Hoeven (ed.), *Exercise of Arms*, pp. 69–113 and 104–105; Parker, *The Army of Flanders*, p.23.

treatises on a scale not seen anywhere else in Europe.[38] As such Spanish commanders were fully aware of the latest tactical developments and the decisive role of firearms.[39] Indeed, Martín de Eguiluz's 1586 treatise *Milicia, Discurso y Regla Militar* described countermarch volley-fire before its supposed introduction by the Dutch.[40]

Overall the *Discourse* reveals a man experienced in the latest tactics as practised by the Spanish Army of Flanders, which in no way lagged behind contemporary European military science. He was well versed in the practicalities of command and showed an appreciable knowledge of siege-craft and fortifications. However, his experience and those of his fellow Irishmen was based on warfare as practised in the Low Countries, which was heavily shaped by siege warfare and not set piece battles.[41] The question was therefore whether this knowledge could be applied to other theatres of war.

The Irish Rebellion

With the completion of his *Discourse* in 1635 Barry returned to Ireland in order to raise a tercio of 2,000 men on behalf of his kinsman John Barry; however, in the event recruitment was never carried out.[42] Three years later, both Tyrone's Tercio, and that of Hugh Albert O'Donnell Earl of Tyrconnell, which had been raised in the Low Countries in 1632, were sent to northern Spain in anticipation of a French attack across the Pyrenees. Serving as sergeant-major (*Sargento mayor*) and effective commander of both Irish tercios, Barry fought at the relief of the Basque port of Fuenterrabía (now Hondarribia) under the overall command of Juan Alfonso Enríquez de Cabrera, Admiral of Castile.[43] As was now typical of Barry, he displayed his accustomed bravery and was instrumental in capturing three French fortifications.[44]

In 1641 Barry was back in Ireland, this time to raise a regiment for Spanish service out of the Earl of Strafford's 9,000 strong Irish Catholic army which had been raised to invade Scotland, but which had subsequently been ordered to disband.[45] On 7 May these men were placed under the command of Barry and seven other officers with

38 De León, *The Road to Rocroi*, p.123.

39 Roberts, *Pike and Shot Tactics*, p.28.

40 Marjolein t'Hart, *The Dutch Wars of Independence. Warfare and Commerce in the Netherlands, 1570–1680* (London: Routledge, 2014), p.64 and Fernando G. de León, 'Spanish Military Power and the Military Revolution', in G. Mortimer (ed.), *Early Modern Military History, 1450–1815* (Basingstoke: Palgrave Macmillan, 2004), pp.25–43, at p.34.

41 Padraig Lenihan, *Confederate Catholics at War 1641–1649* (Cork: Cork University Press, 2001), p.215.

42 De Mesa, *The Irish in the Spanish Armies*, p.49.

43 De Mesa, 'The Irish "nation"', p.166; De Mesa, *The Irish in Spanish Armies*, pp.144–147; Moisés E. Rodriguez, 'The Spanish Habsburgs and their Irish Soldiers (1587–1700)' in *Irish Migration Studies in Latin America* 5/2 (2007), pp.125–130, p.128.

44 De Mesa, 'Gerat Barry', p.156.

45 William Kelly, 'James Butler, the Irish Government, and the Bishops' Wars', in J.R. Young, *Celtic Dimensions of the British Civil Wars* (Edinburgh: John Donald Publishers Ltd, 1997), pp.35–52, 37–39, and 42–43; Ian Gentles, *The English Revolution and the Wars of the Three Kingdoms 1638–1652* (London: Routledge, 2014), pp.50–51; Bartlett and Jeffrey, *A Military History*, p.163.

the intention of sending them to Spain.[46] The following month official contracts were signed but to the consternation of all involved the enterprise was blocked at the beginning of August by the Irish Parliament, who were fearful of providing aid to a Catholic power.[47] In response, and desperate for Spanish financial aid Charles I wrote to the Lords Justices in Dublin requesting that 4,000 soldiers under colonels Gerat Barry, John Barry, George Porter and Theobold Taffe be granted permission to leave for Spain. However, despite Charles's plea the Irish Parliament remained intransigent.[48] Consequently, when the rebellion broke out on 22nd October Barry's regiment was awaiting embarkation near Kinsale.

Having taken the government completely by surprise, the rebel priority was to make rapid gains before effective resistance could be organised.[49] Beginning in Ulster the insurgents under Sir Phelim O'Neill, who had been gathering men under the pretext of sending them to Spain, quickly captured Armagh, Charlemont, Mountjoy Castle, Tandragee and Newry.[50] As the rebellion spread outside of Ulster the Lords Justices in Dublin were anxious to disband the Irish regiments which were still waiting to be given passage to the Continent. Barry and the 1,000 men under his command who were waiting embarkation at Kinsale refused, and lacking men the government was in no position to use force.[51] Rather than risking an assault on the town, Barry moved out of Kinsale in orderto join with other rebel forces assembling in the region. In an effort to secure as much of the country as possible the government garrisoned a number of key ports over the winter months including Cork, Drogheda and Dublin whilst at the same time 4,000 Ulster English and Scots settlers secured Enniskillen, Derry and Belfast.[52] Although some towns, particularly those along the coast such as Limerick, Galway, Waterford (Duncannon Fort) and Kinsale (Castle Park) received modern artillery fortifications, the cost, as Barry had noted in his *Discourse* was ruinously

46 De Mesa, *The Irish in Spanish Armies* p.123.

47 Robert P. Mahaffy, *Calendar of State Papers Relating to Ireland of the Reign of Charles I 1633–1647.* (London, 1901), p.330, and Gentles *The English Revolution*, p.51.

48 Mahaffy, *Calendar of State Papers* p.331; De Mesa, *The Irish in the Spanish Armies*, p.126, and Robert Stradling, *The Spanish Monarchy and Irish Mercenaries: The Wild Geese in Spain 1618–68* (Dublin: Irish Academic Press, 1994), p.33. In the event only 300 men under George Porter reached Spain.

49 Micheál O'Siochru, 'Atrocity, Codes of Conduct and the Irish in the Civil Wars 1641–1653', *Past and Present*, Vol. 195, Issue 1 (2007), pp.55–86 p.59; Gentles, *The English Revolution*, pp.48–50.

50 Gentles, *The English Revolution*, p.53; Jane Ohlmeyer, 'The Civil War in Ireland', in J. Kenyon, J. Ohlmeyer (eds.), *The Civil Wars. A Military History of England, Scotland and Ireland 1638–1660* (Oxford: Oxford University Press, 1998), p.73; Elaine Murphy, 'Siege of Duncannon Fort in 1641 and 1642', in E. Darcy, A. Margey and E. Murphy (eds.), *The 1641 Depositions and the Irish Rebellion* (London: Routledge, 2016), p.144.

51 Mahaffy, *Calendar of State Papers*, p.351, and Lenihan, *Conquest and Resistance*, p.45.

52 Scott Wheeler, 'Four Armies in Ireland', in J.H. Ohlmeyer (ed.), *Ireland, from Independence to Occupation 1641–1660* (Cambridge: Cambridge University Press, 1995), pp.43–66, at p.44.

expensive.[53] Consequently by the eve of the rebellion many defences, including those of Dublin, were in a poor state of repair.[54]

As news of the rising spread, it was not long before other Continental veterans began to make their way back to Ireland. Anxious to prevent the arrival of men and supplies, orders were issued by the government to intercept or detain vessels suspected of providing aid to the insurgents.[55] Although these veterans only made up a small percentage of soldiers in the Confederate armies, they played a disproportionately large role in sergeant-major appointments.[56] Responsible for training new recruits, the knowledge they contributed was vital considering the majority of men were inexperienced and had been levied either as volunteers or through impressment.[57] Some of the troops under Barry's command, had been raised as part of Strafford's 'New Army' and formed the backbone of the new Confederate army. Properly trained and equipped, their commander St Leger noted they were 'not ... poor stinking rascally sneaks thes are brave gallant fellows ... there clothes are better, theire persons better and there mettel is better.'[58] However, the majority of recruits were inexperienced and in some cases lacked conventional weaponry.[59] Whilst aiming to equip their men with pikes and muskets at a ratio of 2:1, the high cost of gunpowder meant that some armies, such as that of Munster, lacked firearms.[60] Indeed, the limited supply of gunpowder, which had previously been obtained from England, seriously affected the Confederate war effort in 1642.

Despite the disadvantages Barry's first task, as recently appointed commander of the Irish forces in Munster (comprising the counties of Clare, Limerick, Tipperary, Waterford, Cork and Kerry), was to besiege Cork along with Lord Muskerry, in order to prevent the port from being used to land supplies and reinforcements from England.[61] Given Barry's previous experience of siege warfare, in theory at least, the operation should have been a success. However, according to Richard Bellings, secretary to the Irish Confederation, Barry was woefully underprepared; possessing just 50 horse and

53 Rolf Loeber and Geoffrey Parker, 'The Military Revolution in Seventeenth Century Ireland', in J.H. Ohlmeyer, *Ireland from Independence to Occupation, 1641 1660*, pp.68–70; J.H. Ohlmeyer, 'The Wars of Religion 1603–1610', in Bartlett and Jeffrey, p.161.

54 J.H. Ohlmeyer, 'The Wars of Religion', p.161, and Ronald Hutton and Wylie Reeves, 'Sieges and Fortifications', in Kenyon and Ohlmeyer, *The Civil Wars*, pp.202–203.

55 Elaine Murphy, *Ireland and the War at Sea 1641–1653* (Woodbridge: Boydell, 2012), p.20.

56 Lenihan, *Confederate Catholics*, pp.44–45.

57 Lenihan, *Confederate Catholics*, pp.44–45; Padraig Lenihan, 'Conclusions: Ireland's Military Revolution(s)', in P. Lenihan, *Conquest and Resistance. War in Seventeenth-Century Ireland* (Leiden: Brill, 2001), pp.345–371, at p.353.

58 Quoted in Bartlett and Jeffrey, p.163, and Stradling, *The Spanish Monarchy*, p.90.

59 Padraig Lenihan, '"Celtic" Warfare in the 1640s', in Young, *Celtic Dimensions*, pp.120–121, and Sean J. Connolly, *Divided Kingdom. Ireland 1630–1800* (Oxford: Oxford University Press, 2008), p.65.

60 J.H. Ohlmeyer, 'The Wars of Religion', p.172; Donal O'Carroll, 'Change and Continuity in Weapons and Tactics 1594–1691', in P. Lenihan, *Conquest and Resistance. War in Seventeenth-Century Ireland* (Leiden: Brill, 2001), pp.221–257, p.233.

61 Wiggins, *Anatomy of a siege*, p.48, and J.J. Gilbert (ed.), *History of the Irish Confederation and the War in Ireland 1641–1643* (Dublin, 1882), pp.73.

1.3 Murrough O'Brien 1st Earl of Inchiquin by John Michael Wright *c.*1660–1670. (Image courtesy of Manchester Art Gallery Acc. 1945.225)

3,000 'ill-armed' infantry. Lacking sufficient troops to fully invest the city he was unable to prevent Sir Charles Vavasour from soon reinforcing the city with 1,000 men and much needed supplies.[62] Following a number of weeks of relative inaction, the malaise was eventually broken when Barry sent forward 200 men with the intent of provoking a sally from the city. Unfortunately for the Confederates the tactic worked too well. Under the command of the young and vigorous Continental veteran Murrough O'Brien, Baron Inchiquin, 400 musketeers and three troops of horse firstly pushed back Barry's advance party before engaging with the main Confederate force. After a brief but determined resistance, Inchiquin's forces managed to overrun and complete disperse the Confederates, capturing their baggage in the process. For Bellings, the reason for the defeat was Barry's lack of experience directing such operations in an environment very different to that of Flanders. Whilst this explanation certainly cannot be ignored,

62 Gilbert, *History of the Irish Confederation*. pp.74–75.

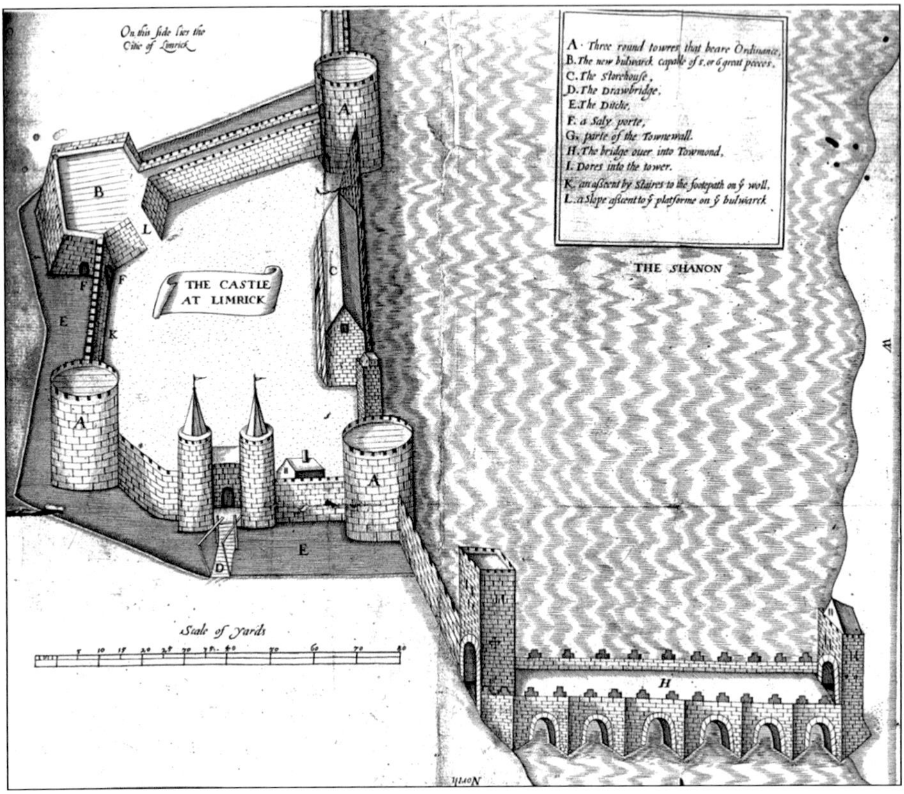

1.4 Plan of King John's Castle Limerick, reproduced from J. Ferrar's *History of Limerick*, 1787. Note the bulwark marked 'B'. (Image courtesy of Limerick City & County Library)

there were undoubtedly other contributory factors. In particular the relatively small size of his army together with its limited resources, especially gunpowder, meant that Barry faced a considerable challenge. Certainly the judgement that Barry delayed operations in order to draw as much pay (£3 per day) from the Council of War as possible is difficult to reconcile with the decorated Continental veteran.[63]

With Cork remaining in enemy hands, the Munster Confederates moved on to Limerick; the third largest urban centre in Ireland. Having been admitted into the city sometime between 1 and 15 May by the sympathetic mayor Dominick Fanning, Barry proceeded to lay siege to the castle which held out under George Courtenay.[64] Unlike at Cork, the possession of the city with its buildings providing both shelter from enemy fire and vantage points over the castle, gave the Confederates a considerable advantage.

63 Quoted in Gilbert, *History of the Irish Confederation*, pp.75.
64 Wiggins, *Anatomy of a Siege*, pp.67–72 at p.89 n23; Gilbert, *History of the Irish Confederation*, p. liiii.

Perhaps feeling more secure, Barry prosecuted the siege in a manner one would expect of a veteran of this mode of warfare. To begin with every effort had to be made to prevent supplies from reaching the city. Consequently, a boom was constructed across the Shannon and a number of forts erected along its banks to harass enemy shipping.[65] Barry's most pressing concern, however, was his lack of siege artillery. Although his army possessed 11 field pieces the largest, a demi-culverin, was quite ineffective against the stone defences of King John's Castle.[66] Conversely, whilst the castle's garrison possessed six pieces of ordnance which included a mighty 32 lb demi-cannon, they were unable to capitalise on their advantage due to their limited supplies of gunpowder.[67] Consequently, lacking suitable siege artillery or enough men for a direct assault, and fearful that relief ships would ultimately break through the cordon, it was decided the only way to capture the castle was by mining.[68] Among the Confederates it is likely that Barry was the only individual who was experienced in siege-craft having witnessed mining operations most recently at Fuenterrabía. However, lacking the specialist knowledge of an engineer – his *Discourse* does not contain a section on mining operations – the mines relied on the old-fashioned burnt-prop method rather than explosive charges.[69] Arguably though, against the largely medieval defences of the castle (a single projecting bastion or 'bulwarck' had been constructed by Sir Josias Bodley in 1611), nothing more was needed. Indeed, though forced by necessity, the endeavour paid off. On 23 June after weeks of difficult and dangerous work and with the eastern curtain wall and the modern bastion severely damaged, Courtenay had little option but to surrender the castle.[70] Suffering relatively few casualties, Limerick was a major triumph, providing the Confederates a secure base in Munster.

Wasting no time, the castle's ordnance was dismounted and added to the Confederates' artillery train. With the three-ton demi-cannon mounted on a hollowed-out tree trunk to prevent it from sinking in soft ground and dragged by a team of 25 oxen, Barry possessed the largest mobile gun in the country.[71] Over the coming weeks, numerous garrisons surrendered on sight of the Confederate forces as they moved towards Cork.[72] On 30 August Barry's forces arrived before Liscarroll Castle, which although described as being 'strong both by art and nature', was garrisoned by only 30 men. Unsurprisingly, given the artillery and number of men arrayed against them, the garrison surrendered

65 Lenihan, 'Barry, Gerat' p.131.

66 Wiggins, *Anatomy of a Siege*, p.73.

67 Murphy, *Ireland and the War at Sea*, p.21; Lenihan, *Confederate Catholics*, p.57, and Thomas Carte, *An History of the Life of James Duke of Ormonde From his Birth in 1610 to his Death in 1688. Volume 1* (London, 1736), p.341.

68 Wiggins, *Anatomy of a Siege*, p.87.

69 Wiggins, *Anatomy of a Siege*, p.220.

70 Wiggins, *Anatomy of a Siege*, pp.170–174.

71 Lenihan, *Confederate Catholics*, p.57; Padraig Lenihan, *Consolidating Conquest: Ireland 1603–1627* (London: Routledge, 2007), p.112; Wiggins, *Anatomy of a Siege*, p.226; Carte, *An History*, pp.341–343.

72 Lenihan, *Confederate Catholics*, p.57 and Carte, *An History* p.343

three days later.[73] Meanwhile Lord Inchiquin had gathered a force of 2,000 foot and 400 horse and marched towards the castle where he found the Confederates arrayed in good order on rising ground.[74] Outnumbering the enemy by possibly as many as 4,000 or 5,000 men, the Confederate army was divided into 'three great bodies', primarily composed of pikemen, with the left wing and artillery anchored on the castle and the right wing, including the cavalry, on recently erected (siege?) fortifications. Faced with attacking uphill against defended positions, Inchiquin's primary concern was to draw the Confederates down to lower ground. However, his initial advance was beaten back by a body of musketeers which had taken up position in a ditch in advance of the main Confederate lines. Meanwhile Barry's artillery had opened up on Inchiquin's forces, yet despite the havoc they could have wrought, they 'were planted too high and did little mischief'. Consequently, Inchquin was able to array his forces into battle lines and begin the main assault. Initially the Confederate horse performed well by beating back Inchiquin's cavalry and threatening to win the day. Nonetheless, they soon demonstrated their indiscipline by breaking formation and dispersing over the battlefield, thus allowing Inchiquin to reform his men and defeat them piecemeal. With their cavalry beaten, it was not long before the right wing of the Confederate infantry collapsed, shortly followed by the left and centre. Given the advantage of numbers and terrain Barry's forces should have emerged victorious. However, the ineffectual performance of his artillery, the indiscipline of his men and his failure to coordinate his troops allowed the tactically astute Inchiquin to turn what may initially have been defeat, into victory.

Although Barry retained nominal command of the Confederate forces in Munster after the battle, his reputation was irreparably damaged.[75] The following year James Tuchet Earl of Castlehaven defeated Sir Charles Vavasour at Cloghlia with speedy use of his horse; recapturing the Limerick ordnance which Barry had lost at Liscarroll.[76] Following the cessation of hostilities in September 1643 Barry was largely forgotten and became 'more like a countrie boore than a martiall generall'.[77] Barry died, probably around the age of 60, in Limerick city in early March 1646.[78]

Conclusion

Without doubt Barry's experiences on the Continent had not fully equipped him to meet all the challenges of war in Ireland. In addition, by the time he led the army of Munster, he was over fifty, and lacked the vigour shown by younger men like Inchiquin. Nevertheless his successful operations from Limerick to Liscarroll demonstrated that despite the lack of men and equipment he was a resourceful commander; competent

73 Wiggins, *Anatomy of a Siege* p.226

74 James Grove White, *Historical and Topographical Notes etc on Buttevant, Castletownroche, Doneraile, Mallow and places in their vicinity. Volume IV* (Cork, 1916). p.28 and Carte, *An History*, p.343.

75 Wiggins, *Anatomy of a Siege*, p.227.

76 Touchet, *The memoirs of James, Lord Audley*, pp.57–62.

77 Quoted in Wiggins, *Anatomy of a Siege*, p.227.

78 Lenihan, 'Barry, Gerat', p.131.

in the difficulties of siege warfare. This 'qualitative edge in siegecraft', was certainly shared by his by his fellow veterans Owen Roe O'Neill and Thomas Preston, who had been appointed commanders of the Ulster and Leinster forces respectively.[79] Like Barry, both had seen extensive service on the Continent and had fought alongside each other at Breda. The battlefield success of the Confederates was, however, decidedly less impressive. As such, rather than viewing Barry's defeat at Liscarroll in isolation it is worth remembering that of all the major battles fought between 1641 and 1653, only Benburb was a success.[80] Here a much superior army, recruited and equipped from money and arms given by the Papal nuncio Giovani Battista Rinuccini, and commanded by Spanish-trained officers including O'Neill, decisively defeated the 'united British Protestant forces' under Robert Monro.[81]

Although many issues hampered Barry and the Confederate cause in general, one major drawback was their lack of cavalry. After all, it was Inchiquin's superior cavalry which had played such a decisive role in Barry's defeats at Cork and Liscarroll. Although the Irish cavalry was generally of good quality, the lack of suitable horses and the overall high cost of equipment meant that recruiting sufficient numbers remained a serious problem.[82] Consequently, the Confederates lacked tactical flexibility in a period when this was becoming increasingly important. However, even with more cavalrymen at their disposal, neither Barry, O'Neill or Preston were experienced in cavalry warfare and it is therefore difficult to know if they would have used them effectively. Indeed, Barry himself, although acknowledged the use of cavalry, particularly in reconnaissance, favoured the infantry, observing that 'amonge the antiente Romaines there foote of more estimation then there horse, allwayes houldinge a true opinion, that the Infanterie well disciplined is the right sinue of the warr, the walles of the city and fortress of the realme'.[83] Although conservative in light of the many tactical developments which had emerged during the Thirty Years' War, Barry's high opinion of the pike was shared by many of his contemporaries.[84] Given his experience in Flanders, where cavalry played a comparatively minor role, this is not altogether surprising. Unfortunately, for Barry, this was not true for Ireland.

Whilst Barry and his contemporaries were better suited to siege warfare than open battle, their knowledge of military discipline and experience in the Army of Flanders did

79 Ohlmeyer, *Making Ireland English*, p.271, and Padraig Lenihan, 'Conclusions: Ireland's Military Revolution(s)', in Padraig Lenihan (ed.), *Conquest and Resistance* (Leiden: Brill, 2001), pp.345–371 at p.353.

80 O'Carroll, 'Change and Continuity', pp.221–257 at p.235; Ohlmeyer, *The Civil Wars in Ireland*, pp.81–82; John J. McDonnell, 'Another Look at the Battle of Benburb', in *Seanchas Ardmhacha: Journal of the Armagh Diocesan Historical Society. Volume 9 No. 2* (1979), pp.362–390 p.362.

81 Wheeler, 'Four Armies in Ireland', pp.54–55, and Gerard A. Hayes-McCoy, *Irish Battles. A Military History of Ireland* (Appletree Press, 1990), pp.182 and 185–197.

82 O'Carroll, 'Change and Continuity', pp.235, and Padraig Lenihan, '"Celtic" Warfare in the 1640s', in Young, *Celtic Dimensions*, pp.116–141 at p.134.

83 Barry, *A discourse*, pp.144, 148.

84 Roger Boyle, *A Treatise of the Art of War* (London, 1677), p.24, and see Donald Lupton, *A Warre-like Treatise of the Pike* (London, 1642).

have a significant transformative effect on the Confederate armies. Their appreciation of military theory, the latest technological developments and practical battlefield experience resulted in Confederate tactics conforming more closely to the latest Continental models.[85] As Ulster commissioner Sir Arthur Annesley and Irish politician Sir William Parsons admitted in 1646 the Irish 'have their men in a better order or warr and better commanded by captains of experience and practice of warr then ever they were since the conquest.'[86]

Acknowledgements

My thanks to Dr Padraig Lenihan, National University of Ireland, Galway, and Dr Eduardo de Mesa for their advice and assistance and making a number of useful suggestions to an early draft of the text. Thanks also to Stuart Ivinson, Librarian at the Royal Armouries Leeds, for obtaining many of the sources cited in this article.

85 Lenihan, *Consolidating Conquest*, p.132, and Ó Siochrú 'Atrocity, Codes of Conduct', pp.55–86 at p.64.
86 Quoted Loeber and Parker, 'The Military Revolution', p.88.

2

Aston, Butler and Murray

British Officers in the Service of Polish Vasa Kings 1621–1634

Michał Paradowski

'There came 150 Scots, good faith [Catholic] lads, seems [they] have more bravery and eagerness that German [soldiers]. They immediately mustered in front of the King [Stephen Bathory]. If we would have a few thousand like them, we could attack Pskov's walls.'[1] This description from October 1581 is one of the many first-hand accounts of Poles and Lithuanians impressed with the military prowess of Scottish, English and Irish mercenaries serving during the numerous wars waged by Polish–Lithuanian Commonwealth in the 16th and 17th centuries. Such soldiers were especially frequent 'visitors' during the reign of Sigismund III (between 1587 and 1632) and his son Władysław IV (between 1632 and 1648). It was turbulent time for the Commonwealth, with fighting against Turks, Tatars, Muscovites, Swedes and Cossacks. In this paper I would like to focus on the period 1621–1634 in an attempt to present the life and deeds of three soldiers that arrived from the British Isles and fought for Polish Vasa kings.

There are a few reasons why I decided to focus on those specific officers. The primary one is their nationality: Arthur Aston was English, James Butler was Irish and James Murray was Scottish.[2] During 1621–1634 they often served in the same theatre of war, so it is more than probable that they personally knew each other. There are a fair number of primary sources where their names and actions are mentioned,[3] which allows us to draw some proper timeline of their service. Finally, the end of their Polish

1 Jan Piotrowski, *Dziennik wyprawy Stefana Batorego pod Psków* (Kraków, 1894), p. 134.

2 Unfortunately I was not able to identify any officer of Welsh origin.

3 Interestingly enough, Butler's name is often written down as Putler, while Murray appears as More, Moore and Mora.

service had very distinct conclusions, so it will be interesting to present their attempts to gain glory, fame and wealth during the Polish wars.

While we will focus on the period 1621–1634, it is important to state that for two of those officers service in Poland started earlier. Murray appears as a courtier to Sigismund III in either 1601 or 1603, and in 1609 we see him as Stuart's envoy to Poland.[4] Butler served, in charge of 100 men of foreign infantry, during Royal Prince Władysław's attempt to capture the Muscovite throne in 1617.[5] He took part in an unsuccessful assault on Moscow on 10–11 October 1618,[6] and seems to have left a very good impression on the future Polish king. He was then allowed to return to the British Isles, to recruit more troops. He returned with them in 1621. It was an important time for the Commonwealth, as a new war, this time against the Ottoman Turks, started the previous year. In September 1620 the Polish army, led by Grand Hetman Stanisław Żółkiewski and Field Hetman Stanisław Koniecpolski, was defeated by the Turks and Tatars at Cecora in Moldavia and forced to retreat. On 6 October, when the retreating Polish army arrived near Mohyłów, approximately 10 km from the border river of Dniester, demoralised troops broke their ranks and started to flee towards the river, leading to total disaster and the massacre of the Polish army. Żółkiewski died in a heroic last stand, Koniecpolski and many of his officers were captured and spent the next few years as Turkish prisoners.

In January 1621 Jerzy Ossoliński, royal courtier and trusted advisor of Sigismund III, was sent to London with the mission of obtaining James I's support against the Turks. The Polish king provided his envoy with long and detailed instructions, with the main point being to ask James' permission to recruit 8,000 infantry, suggesting 'let England provide [us] with men experienced in warfare, Scotland gallant and Ireland brave ones.' Ossoliński was also to seek financial and diplomatic assistance, hoping that James could help to negotiate a truce or even peace between the Poles and Turks. The Polish envoy made a good impression on both James and his royal advisor George Villiers but negotiations – especially those regarding financial aid – were extremely slow. There seem to have been plenty of volunteers that wanted to serve against the Turks, however, and Ossoliński made a rather interesting comment about them, writing that 'my opinion is that Irish are the best, as they are tough and [are] good Catholics; Scots are also tough but they are really serious heretics. Amongst the English [there are] plenty of Catholics but [they are] soft.'[7] The biggest problem however was connected with the choice of the correct officers to lead the recruitment effort. Ossoliński had some reservations about the two main candidates, Sir Arthur Aston Senior and Sir Robert Stuart. 'As Aston is English, Scots may not

4 Anna Biegańska, 'Żołnierze szkoccy w dawnej Rzeczpospolitej', *Studia i Materiały do Historii Wojskowości*, volume XXVII, Warszawa 1984, p. 95.

5 Jakub Sobieski, *Diariusz ekspedycyjej moskiewskiej dwuletniej królewicza Władysława 1617–1618*, (Opole, 2010), p. 34.

6 *Ibid.*, p. 77.

7 *Jerzego Ossolińskiego, kanclerza wielkiego koronnego autobiografia* (Lwów, 1876), p. 141.

want to go with him, [while] Stuart is born Scot, [so] English and Irish won't go with him.'[8] Finally Aston was chosen, who had previous experience of service in Poland and Muscovy but was also Catholic, which make him much more trustworthy in Polish eyes. Here is when Aston Jr, one of our three main characters, enters the scene. He was sent as his father's envoy to Poland, delivering Ossoliński's letters to Warsaw, then bringing back Sigismund's answer to London.

Later he led the first wave of recruited troops, by mid September 1621 arriving in Gdańsk with approximately 300 men. Soon afterwards his father, with a much smaller unit, also reached Poland. Unfortunately for the Poles, that was all the soldiers that arrived. Further ships, transporting companies raised in England and Ireland, were stopped by the Danes and never reached their destination. Some soldiers returned to England where their companies were disbanded, others chose service in Flanders instead. In overall, the whole Ossoliński–Aston mission brought very small reinforcements, that arrived far too late, as since 2 September 1621 the Polish–Lithuanian army was already besieged by the Turks in Chocim (Khotyn) and no troops could be sent to them.

There was a new war theatre where British soldiers could be sent, however. In August 1621 Swedish King Gustav II Adolf landed with a large army in Livonia. After less than a month's siege, the most important port in the region, Riga, was finally captured by the Swedes – a feat that they could not achieve during the 1600–1611 war. A small Lithuanian army led by Hetman Krzysztof II Radziwiłł was not able to prevent it, and could only harass the Swedish troops as part of 'small war' efforts. In January 1622, taking advantage of the fact that Gustav Adolf was back in Sweden and his troops were located in winter quarters, Radziwiłł besieged the capital of Courland, Mitawa (Mitau), captured by the Swedes in October 1621. The Lithuanian hetman desperately needed more troops, especially infantry, so he sent letter after letter to Warsaw, urging for new reinforcements. In late January 1622 two units of infantry were sent out to join Radziwiłł's army: Aston with 400 men and Butler with 300.[9] Three official army records from that time mentioned both units as 300 men each,[10] so it is possible that hetman's envoy had some wrong information or (less likely) that Aston lost 100 men en route to Courland. On 12 February 1622[11] both units arrived at Lithuanian camp, joining the troops besieging Mitau. Butler raised the spirit of Radziwiłł's troops, leading his soldiers in an impromptu parade through the city market, facing the guns in the Swedish garrison.[12] Both officers were called 'captains of His Royal Highness' and their units became officially part of the Lithuanian army

8 Wacław Borowy, 'Anglicy, Szkoci i Irlandczycy w wojsku polskim za Zygmunt III' in H. Barycz, J. Hulewicz (eds.), *Studia z dziejów kultury polskiej* (Warszawa, 1949), p. 305.

9 Archiwum Główne Akt Dawnych w Warszawie (AGAD), AR V 12789/I, p. 133. J. Frąckiewicz Radzyminski do K. II. Radziwiła, Warszawa 25 I 1622.

10 AGAD f. 354, Dział II nr 799, Wykaz woyska Jego Królewskiej Mości wysłanego do Inflant.

11 Some sources also give the date as the 10th or 11th.

12 AGAD, AR V, nr 6956, p. 16, Piotr Kochowski to Krzysztof II Radziwiłł, 12 II 1622, Mitau.

camped near Mitau. British soldiers were immediately thrown into the fight, as the Hetman believed he was on the verge of breaking the defenders' resolve. Two weeks later, in his letter to Sigismund, he highly praised the new arrivals, 'captain Aston shown exemplary courage and hopefully he will be so eager [to fight] until the end of his service. But I can also see that captain Putler does not lack [courage] on each occasion [of fighting].'[13] Butler reported to Radziwiłł, that while in Poland he was also offered to raise a unit of 150 dragoons, so the Hetman asked Sigismund to issue an official document, as 'such troops will be needed in his army' and that the Irish officer was a very good candidate to be in charge of them.[14]

The siege of Mitau dragged on until summer 1622. Finally, the decimated Swedish garrison surrendered on 5 July. The relief force, led by Gustav Adolf himself, arrived 11 days too late. For the next three weeks, Swedish and Lithuanian forces were locked in small-scale fighting around Mitau, focused on bitter fighting for field fortifications built by the Lithuanians during the siege. Aston, Butler and their troops were in the thick of the fight, facing much stronger Swedish infantry. Both sides were in fact exhausted due to the long campaign, so finally on 10 August Lithuanian and Swedish envoys signed a truce, that was to be effective until May 1623.

The majority of the Lithuanian army, including foreign infantry, was disbanded by the end of 1622. Both Aston and Butler seem to have been retained in service, as they were part of the group of 13 officers and cavalry companions that on 6 March 1623 presented in front of the King and *Sejm* (parliament) Swedish standards captured during the war. The Hetman also highly praised them for their valiant military service.[15] Both officers then switched to Polish service, probably thanks to recommendation from Radziwiłł. King Sigismund was drawing up plans to prepare for the invasion of Sweden: building a fleet in Gdańsk and recruiting foreign troops, so he was in dire need of good officers that could lead them. In early October 1623 Aston was sent to England, to buy or hire ships. At the end of November the same year Butler sailed to Ireland, to raise a large number of troops.[16]

Aston was retained on royal service, with his troops paid directly from the royal treasury. It was a strong unit, 500 men, who were initially designated to fight as 'marines' on ships. Once the Swedes attacked Livonia in 1625, there was a plan to send Aston and his infantry to support the Lithuanians. For some reason, however, the soldiers stayed in Prussia, so they were available to fight against the Swedes once Gustav Adolf decided to switch his interest from Livonia to Prussia. At the same time we can find Butler in charge of 400 dragoons, as part of the Polish army fighting in September–October 1625 against the Cossacks, then in the summer of 1626 in

13 *Księcia Krzysztofa Radziwiłła hetmana polnego Wielkiego Księstwa Litewskiego sprawy wojenne i polityczne 1621–1632* (Paryż, 1859), p. 160.

14 *Ibid.*, pp. 161–162.

15 *Ibid.*, p. 459.

16 Władysław Czapliński, 'Cień Polski nad Sundem', *Kwartalnik Historyczny*, R. 86, nr 2 (Warszawa, 1979), p. 330.

military demonstration against the Tatars. When Hetman Stanisław Koniecpolski was ordered to relocate the majority of his troops to Prussia, Butler's dragoons marched in the vanguard of this force and at the end of October arrived in the new theatre of war.

Aston and his company, described as '500 Scottish infantry',[17] took part in the battle of Gniew, between 22 September and 1 October 1626. They received special praise for their efforts during the fighting on 22 September, where the company was one of the main 'foreign' units fighting against the Swedish attack. The unit took heavy losses, however, when 'two barrels [of powder] were set on fire by Aston's infantrymen, when they were running with burning match in one hand and recklessly taking powder to the hat [held in] the other.'[18] Up to 30 soldiers were wounded but according to eyewitness none of Aston's soldiers died in the explosion.

In the meantime Murray was already engaged in building the Royal Fleet. In 1620 we can see him appointed as a 'trusted royal servant, with good knowledge of naval architecture' to work as *servitor architectus navalis* (senior naval architect) in the port of Gdańsk.[19] His annual pay was due to be 420 florins and the first ship built under his supervision – *Gelbe Löw*[20] – was ready in 1622. Another document, this time from April 1626, confirmed that his appointment is still in place and raised his pay to 500 florins.[21] His hands were full, as he was commissioned to build 10 more warships. Additionally, probably sometime in early 1626, he received a military patent and as captain raised a company of German infantry. The unit started its service in August 1626, with 'paper strength' of 200 men. Once the Swedes landed in Prussia and the Royal Fleet was mobilised to oppose them, Murray was nominated as captain of the galleon *König David*, one of the two largest ships in the fleet. He took part in the siege of Puck (December 1626–April 1627), with his galleon being part of a squadron assisting land forces. It appears that Aston's unit was present as well, as both companies became part of the Polish garrison afterwards. Butler's dragoons arrived with Hetman Koniecpolski's main forces in March 1627 and after the Swedes surrendered on 2 April 1627, it was the Irishman's unit that escorted them to Tczew.[22] Afterwards Butler's unit took part in a victorious battle against Swedish troops marching from Mecklenburg at Czarne (Hammerstein), that took place between 12 and 18 April same year.[23] Later the same spring dragoons were part of the Polish army besieging

17 Archiwum Państwowe w Gdańsku, dział 48, nr 300,53, Diariusz Wojny Pruskiej z roku 1626, p.344.
18 *Ibid.*, pp.360–362.
19 AGAD, Metryka Koronna, MK166, p. 210.
20 'Yellow Lion'. All ships of the Royal Fleet were named in German.
21 AGAD, Metryka Koronna, MK 174, p. 153.
22 'Diariusz albo Summa spraw i dzieł wojska kwarcianego w Prusiech na usłudze Jego Królewskiej Miłości przeciwko Gustawowi Książęciu Sudermańskiemu będącego' in Stanisław Przyłęcki (ed.), *Pamiętniki o Koniecpolskich* (Lwów, 1842), p. 20.
23 *Ibid.*, p. 22.

Gniew, protecting a battery of six cannons that managed to heavily damage the city wall and force the Swedish garrison to surrender.[24]

Butler and his unit were again at forefront of the fight at the beginning of June 1627, when they supported Gdańsk's soldiers defending the crossing through the River Vistula at Kiezmark. As one of the Polish officers reported afterwards:

> At dawn of 2nd of June 1627, the enemy, who took position near Danziger Haupt, left with 30 bigger and smaller boats[25] and marched towards our field fortifications near village of Kiezmark, where [our troops] were already alarmed, having four batteries[26] well equipped with cannons and muskets, ready to fight, colonel [James] Butler was there with his men,[27] also well dug in. In the initial wave of [Swedish troops] were the best captains and other officials[28] with Graf von Thurn, in a few boats arriving at the bank and with great power approaching and assaulting our sconces, [manned by] Danzig troops; some [Swedes] breaking through the fence[29] so Colonel Butler had to support [the Danzig troops], then our cannons, ready with grapeshot, started to shoot. And immediately three Swedish boats full of troops were sunk. Graf von Thurn was shot on the spot, the Swedes took his body to Marienburg,[30] Highest Colonel Akler[?] was taken prisoner and sent to Gdańsk. Another Colonel, called Eryk Ponse[?] with 40 and few [killed] the best soldiers left on the battlefield, so our troops took their clothes and chains,[31] dug two holes near Kiezmark and buried them there. Magnus Reutentarch[?] another important colonel, nobody knows where he is, some people said that he withdrew. In total all the best [Swedish] officers were killed, and Gustav [Adolf] standing on the other bank of Vistula river was – in great fury – throwing his soldiers, like a cattle, into the fight, so they could support their comrades.[32]

The Swedish King himself was severely wounded during this skirmish, so his troops did not make another attempt of crossing until he recovered. They attacked again on 14 July, this time Gdańsk's soldiers were supported by Polish infantry sent from the garrison of Puck. Four hundred musketeers were drawn from two units: Lieutenant-Colonel Fridrich Denhoff's and Major Arthur Aston's, with both officers present in charge of the troops. Unfortunately for them, Gdańsk's mercenaries led by Dutch Colonel Liesemann, under cover of darkness, fled from their fortifications, leaving the Polish

24 *Ibid.*, pp.27–28.

25 He used the term 'bat', frequently used for the description of boats used in Prussia. I believe the English equivalent is bateau/batteu.

26 Probably he means four sconces.

27 The letter being written from Gdańsk, means that Butler's dragoons from the regular army were supporting Gdańsk's mercenary troops.

28 'oficiales' in original.

29 Probably means some obstacles.

30 For some time the Poles thought that von Thurn was killed.

31 Probably means jewellery.

32 'Nowiny z Gdańska o porażce Gustawa' in *Starożytności historyczne polskie*, volume I (Kraków, 1840), pp. 234–235.

infantry to face more than 14,000 Swedish soldiers. Denhoff's and Aston's troopers fought bravely, Chancellor Oxenstierna even called them 'the best Polish infantry' but once they were pushed back to sconces previously manned by Liesemann's soldiers they realised that the position was abandoned. Both units surrendered to Swedes, which was a costly blow to Hetman Koniecpolski. The next day he sent some of his officers to Gdańsk, to investigate if Liesemann retreated from his position 'due to an order from City Council or due to his own will and if fear led him to [such] treason.'[33]

Aston was at some point exchanged for a Swedish officer held in Polish captivity, as in December 1627 we can find him negotiating release of his soldiers in further exchange for Swedish soldiers.[34] In the meantime, most likely during the time he spent in captivity, his company ceased to operate as an independent unit and became part of Colonel Gustav Sparre's[35] infantry regiment. What is more interesting, is that Murray's company also joined this regiment, which provided troops to defend the Polish coast, garrison Puck and support the Royal Fleet with infantry. Aston became major and Murray captain of the new regiment, each in command of one company until the end of the war. There is not much military record of the Englishman for next two years. In February 1628 he was one of the officers dealing with prisoner exchanges, when 12 of his troopers captured at Kiezmark returned to the Polish army,[36] then again he dealt with a similar exchange in June 1628[37] – a fairly long time for his soldiers to be kept in captivity. He is also often mentioned in documents regarding English merchants, whose ships were arrested by the Royal Fleet. Aston seems to make a few attempts to negotiate with Royal Commissars on behalf of his compatriots, so their ships and goods could be released from arrest. In September 1628 we can see his company – amongst six other companies of Sparre's regiment – on the diagram presenting the Polish Order of Battle near Grudziądz.[38] While no pitched battle took place at that time, it clearly shows that the majority of Polish infantry was present and ready to fight against the Swedes.

In 1627 Murray was busy in his role of captain in Royal Fleet. In May his *König David* took part in an attack on a Swedish convoy and engaged one of the enemy's galleons, 'their Swedish ship was in fight with our [Polish] one, captained by Mora, [ships] shooting at each other, where we had up to 20 [men] wounded.'[39] When in the

33 'Diariusz albo Summa…', op. cit., pp. 29–30.

34 'Diarum Commissionis Regiae A tertia Novembris Anni MDCXXVII usque ad ultimam Augusti A[nn]o 1628 Conscriptum per Joannem Heppium Secratarium Commissionis' in Wiktor Fenrych (ed.), *Akta i Diariusz Królewskiej Komisji Okrętowej Zygmunta III z lat 1627–1628* (Gdańsk-Gdynia 2001), pp.97–98.

35 A Swedish officer, loyal to Sigismund III.

36 'Diarum Commissionis…', op. cit., pp. 143, 147.

37 *Ibid.*, p. 257.

38 Krigsarkivet, Stockholm, Erik Dalhbergh, Ordre de Bataille 1600–1679 diagram no 56. It is dated 12th September 1628 (O.S.) so according to Polish sources this military demonstration took place 22nd 1628 (N.S.).

39 'Diariusz albo Summa…' op. cit., p. 54.

autumn it was decided that the Poles would attack a smaller Swedish squadron near Gdańsk, Murray was one of the captains nominated into the War Council. It was a group of experienced officers, whose role was to advise and support Polish Admiral Arendt Dickmann, Vice Admiral Herman Witte and the Captain (in charge of infantry stationed on ships) Johann Storck in fleet preparation. However it seems that the Scot took some slight at the fact that, despite his long service, it was not him who was promoted to Admiral or Vice Admiral. When he led *König David* during the battle of Oliwa on 28 November 1627, his actions were far from exemplary. He kept his ship away from the main fight, not providing the support to those Polish galleons that engaged the Swedes – a fight in which both Dickmann and Storck died. The battle was won by the Poles, with Swedish galleon *Tigern* captured and *Solen* blown up by its own crew. Soon after the battle rumours of Murray's (in)actions begun to spread amongst the fleet. At the beginning of December 1627 he accused quartermaster from *König David*, Hans Bartsch, of slander. Allegedly Bartsch was telling people that he knew very well who was responsible for the fact that *König David* did not engage Swedish ships.[40] The Royal Commissars, who were in charge of the fleet's affairs, started an investigation, interviewing crew members. They delayed providing the outcome, however, until they could speak to the new admiral, Herman Witte, who was at that time leading small squadron on the reconnaissance mission. Sadly, Witte's ship, separated from rest of the group, was attacked by Swedish galleons and sunk with the Admiral and the majority of the crew near Öland island. For the time being Murray was still in charge of *König David*. On 18 December 1627 he received permission to take to his home wounded Scottish fleet lieutenant Jacob Lab, captured by the Poles at Oliwa, so he could take care of him during his recovery period. Murray agreed to pay 2,000 German thalars deposit fee for his compatriot.[41] At some point between January and February 1628 Murray's luck turned for the worse – he was expelled from the Polish fleet, after an investigation into his dubious involvement at the battle of Oliwa. He still retained captaincy of the infantry company, as it was completely separate from his rank and role in the Royal Fleet. Through the rest of the war Murray's unit, which as mentioned before was part of Gustav Sparre's regiment, served in Puck's garrison, defending the coast from Swedish attacks.

James Butler was the busiest of all three officers, his dragoons often employed as some sort of 'fire brigade' sent by Hetman Koniecpolski whenever an emergency occurred. They played an important role in the battle of Tczew (Dirschau) 17–18 August 1627, on the first day supporting the withdrawal of Polish cavalry and on the second day defending the camp against marching Swedes. Koniecpolski praised the Irishman in a letter from 19 August writing that 'my brave Butler stands [against the

40 'Diarum Commissionis…', op. cit., p. 86.

41 *Ibid.*, p. 88.

Swedes] in the way that a great Gallant Man should.'[42] Butler's service was awarded, probably mainly due to Hetman Koniecpolski's recommendation and patronage, during the *Sejm* in the autumn of 1627. On 27 November received the highest possible accolade for a foreigner in Polish service, the so-called *indygenat* (grant of nobility to a foreign noble):

> Taking under consideration the brave and full of sacrifice services of Iakub Buthler, Irish noble, that he delivered to Us and to the Commonwealth during different military expeditions, [while] serving faithfully and in such good manner; under agreement from all Polish and Lithuanian states, we take him as *indigena*, [which means he is now] the Commonwealth's noble; under condition that he will give Us his oath of allegiance[43]

While it was rather unusual practice, it seems that in 1628 Butler was in charge of an ad hoc organised combined regiment of infantry and dragoons. There were five companies, varying in size: 147, 149, 200, 300 and 432 (Butler's own) men for total of 1,228 all ranks.[44] As late as 12 December 1628 he received formal commission to raise the regiment, although even this happened in an unusual way. A document was issued to him by Hetman Koniecpolski, not by King Sigismund III.[45] It was not the normal practice, as by law it was the monarch that sent so-called *listy przypowiednie* (recruitment letters) to chosen officers. Nonetheless neither Koniecpolski nor Butler seems to have had any problems due to such activity, which again supports the theory that commission was in fact just the confirmation of the rank and position he held for almost a year. The Irishman spent a large amount of money on organising and equipping his new unit and only in 1635 (*sic*!) was he promised the receipt of that money back.

Butler was very active in his new role, fighting against the Swedish offensive in the summer and autumn of 1628, then again in the winter and the summer of 1629. In August 1628 his regiment was quickly dispatched by Koniecpolski to garrison Grudziądz and prevent Gustav Adolf from capturing it: the infantry was left in town while Butler with dragoons, supported by cossack cavalry, was sent near to Lubawa to

42 Biblioteka Jagiellońska, rkp. 102, III, pp. 1091–1092. Copia Listu JMP Hetmana do P. Starosty Laiskiego zpod Lubieszowa 19 August 1627.

43 *Volumina Legum*, volume III (Petersburg, 1859), p. 265.

44 Biblioteka Czartoryskich 1772, pp. 476–483. Regestrum rationis thesauri Regni in Conventu anni MDCXXIX expeditae. 1629 r.

45 Anna Biegańska, 'Żołnierze szkoccy…' op. cit., p. 94.

harass the Swedes.[46] His whole regiment is then shown on a diagram presenting the Polish order of battle near Grudziądz.[47]

At the end of January 1629 Butler, in command of 800 dragoons and a few hundred infantry,[48] was supporting Polish cavalry fighting with the vanguard of the Swedish army marching to relieve Brodnica. There is no confirmation of whether the Irish colonel and/or his troops took part in the battle of Górzno on 12 February 1629, where the Polish army was defeated and forced to retreat. Butler's dragoons were again in action at the battle of Trzciana on 27 June 1629, when joint Polish and Imperial forces defeated the Swedes led by Gustaf Adolf himself. In the summer of 1629,[49] the regiment had 'paper strength' of 1,037 men in five companies. The actual strength had to be much lower, as the whole Polish army suffered heavily due to combat, sickness, starvation and desertions. In September 1629 during the muster of part of Koniecpolski's army we can find information that 'dragoons in the camps [have paper strength] of 1300 [men] but now on 15th September there are [only] 400 [men mustered].'[50] The final action where we can find Butler and his troops was a night attack on Swedish positions near Malbork, that was attempted from 25–26 July 1629. Units from three 'foreign' infantry regiments, Butler's, Gerhard Denhoff's and Fridrich Denhoff's,[51] supported by some *haiduks*, attacked the Swedish sconces (so called 'small' and 'large') held by the Swedish regiment of Colonel Matts Kagge.[52] The Polish infantry in a heavy fight managed to capture and destroy the 'small' sconce and some units broke through to the forefront of the Swedish camp. The Poles were unable to capture the 'large' sconce however, and after a whole night's fight decided to retreat in the morning. Butler was severely wounded 'in the throat' during attempts to capture the 'large sconce', also one of his captains – Gall – was shot and wounded.[53]

46 'Relacja IMP. Wojewody Sendomirskiego, Hetmana Polnego Koronnego, o wojnie przeszłego roku w Warszawie, dnia 4 Februari 1629 uczyniona' in Otto Laskowski (ed.) *Przyczynki do działań hetmana polnego koronnego Stanisława Koniecpolskiego w Prusach Wschodnich i na Pomorzu przeciwko Gustawowi Adolfowi*, *Przegląd Historyczno-Wojskowy*, volume IX, part 3 (Warszawa, 1937), p. 422; 'Od Pana Hetmana do Pana Starosty Wiskiego, w obozie pod Gniewem, dnia 19 sierpnia 1628' in Stanisław Przyłęcki (ed.), *Pamiętniki o Koniecpolskich* (Lwów, 1842), p. 108; 'Od Pana Hetmana do Króla Jego Mości, w obozie pod Nowem, dnia 21 sierpnia 1628' in Stanisław Przyłęcki (ed.), *Pamiętniki o Koniecpolskich* (Lwów, 1842), p. 109.

47 See footnote 38.

48 Biblioteka Raczyńskich. 75, f. 263–263v, Z listu pułkownika jednego de data 29 januarii.

49 Riksarkivet Stockholm, Extranea 80, Comput Woyska J. K. M. rkps.

50 AGAD, AZ, 3116, p. 12.

51 Ex-Gustav Sparre's regiment. Sparre died 18 July 1629 and was replaced in command by his former Lieutenant-Colonel, Fridrich Denhoff.

52 He died during the fight.

53 'Kontynuacja Diariusza o dalszych postępach wojennych ze Szwedami a die 1 Julii (1629), Przyczynki do działań hetmana polnego koronnego Stanisława Koniecpolskiego w Prusach Wschodnich i na Pomorzu przeciw Gustawowi Adolfowi' in Otto Laskowski (ed.), *Przyczynki do działań hetmana polnego koronnego Stanisława Koniecpolskiego w Prusach Wschodnich i na Pomorzu przeciwko Gustawowi Adolfowi*, *Przegląd Historyczno-Wojskowy*, volume IX, part 3 (Warszawa, 1937), pp. 441–442.

Both sides finally decided to end the war at the negotiators' table. On 16 (26) September 1629 a six-year truce was signed in Stary Targ (Altmark). Soon aftewards the Polish army was largely disbanded, with only the national cavalry and some dragoons sent to Ukraine. Of course it affected our three officers. While Murray seems to remain in Polish service, probably as part of the Royal Household Guard,[54] Aston and Butler chose completely different employment. The Englishman ended up in the service of a former enemy, Gustav Adolf, recruiting in 1631 a foot regiment for the Swedish army. He was never part of the main field army though, and seems to have been deployed in some secondary theatres of war until 1640, when he returned to England. He ended up in the service of Charles I during the English Civil War and died on 11 September 1649 at Drogheda in Ireland. Butler took an Imperial commission and, with the dragoon regiment of former Polish soldiers, went to fight in Wallenstein's army. Probably he did not expect however, that soon he would be back in the service of the new Polish king.

King Sigismund III died in Warsaw on 30 April 1632. The new monarch had to be chosen via free election, which took place between 27 September and 8 November same year, but for a few months the Commonwealth was kingless, with the Primate of Poland, Jan Wężyk, acting *Interrex*. Muscovy, seeing this time as a moment of great vulnerability, decided to invade Lithuania. Tsar Michael I, under the influence of his father, Patriarch Filaret of Moscow, had been preparing his country for war since 1630, negotiating with Sweden, recruiting foreign mercenaries and training its own recruits in Western-style combat. In October 1632 between 20,000 and 30,000 Muscovite soldiers[55] led by Mikhail Borisovich Shein entered Lithuania and marched to besiege Smoleńsk, the key fortress in the region. The Polish–Lithuanian garrison made great efforts to defend the city but it was obvious that without a strong relief force Smoleńsk would not hold forever. Lithuanian Field Hetman Krzysztof II Radziwiłł, leading a small Lithuanian army, began to harass the besiegers but he could not even dream of dislodging the Muscovites from their positions around the city.

The newly elected Polish King, Władysław IV (Sigismund's son), started to prepare a relief force with great energy. Knowing the composition of Muscovite army, with its many Western-type foot regiments and field fortification around Smoleńsk, and drawing from experience of the 1626–1629 war against Sweden, he decided to change the typical model of the Polish army. More than half his force would be composed of infantry, mostly Western-style, and dragoons. The colonel's patents were issued to experienced officers, such as Henryk Denhof, Jakub Weyher or Reinhold Rosen. The King was especially keen on having James Butler back in his service, so he wrote a few letters to Wallenstein, asking for the veteran colonel to be released from Imperial service. Wallenstein not only agreed for that but he also allowed Irishman to take

54 Troops paid directly from the Royal Treasury, that were not part of the standing army.

55 As always sources vary in that particular matter. It is most probable that the initial force numbered just over 20,000 and only with further reinforcements, by the beginning of 1633, did it reach 30,000 soldiers.

with him a 600-strong regiment of dragoons from Silesia.[56] While James was to be nominal colonel of this unit, its field commander became Ernest Alexander Butler. Once he arrived to Poland, James received commission to raise a 1,000-strong foot regiment. He led those two units as part of the royal army, that at the beginning of September 1633 arrived at Radziwiłł's camp near Smoleńsk.

While Władysław IV and his commanders were working on raising and equipping the new Polish army, they did not forgot about Hetman Radziwiłł and his troops. Already in December 1632 he sent to him two companies of his guard dragoons.[57] The captains assigned to lead those soldiers were Murray and Marwitz,[58] and depending on sources they were initially in charge of 250 or 300 men. En route to Radziwiłł's camp they were to recruit their units to total of 400 men, with nominal strength of each company planned as 200 men. The captains did not succeed however, as the total strength of both companies on their arrival to Lithuanian camp was just 291 dragoons.

In March 1633 the royal dragoons, still under the command of Murray and Marwitz, took part in an attempt to break into Smoleńsk, to supply defenders with much needed powder, bullets and money for garrison's delayed pay.[59] Two hundred dragoons and 550 soldiers chosen from winged hussars and cossack cavalry banners, under the overall command of *rittmeister* Jerzy Jurzyc, marched under cover of darkness, while the Muscovites were busy repelling a Lithuanian diversionary assault on their positions. Unfortunately the operation was only partially successful. Many soldiers lost their way in the unfamiliar terrain and only 294 men (including 100 dragoons) managed to reach Smoleńsk. Many others, Murray included, returned to the Lithuanian camp. A group led by Captain Marwitz was scattered by the Muscovites, with many soldiers killed, and others, including Marwitz, being captured. It appears that Murray took over the remnants of both companies and led them during the rest of the campaign.

Butler's regiments, most likely working next to each other throughout the whole campaign, were in the vanguard of the army attempting to break the siege. On 21 September 1633 they took the brunt of the Muscovite counter-attacks, defending small fortifications built in front of Pokrowska Mountain (*Góra Pokrowska*). More than 3,000 of the Muscovite soldiers 'for four hours were giving constant fire [against] Butler.'[60] At some point the Poles were assaulted from two sides, and to make matters even worse three barrels of powder, kept in one of their hastily built blockhouses, exploded, adding to the overall confusion. King Władysław sent reinforcements for

56 It was the only 'Western' unit of Polish army composed of foreigners. All foot regiments and the rest of the dragoons were recruited locally in Poland and Lithuania, with officers and NCOs mostly chosen from amongst the experienced foreigners.

57 Units paid from the King's own treasury.

58 Probably German.

59 Jan Moskorzowski, *Dyariusz wojny moskiewskiej 1633 roku*, Biblioteka Ordynacyi Krasińskich, Muzeum Konstantego Świdzińskiego, volume 13 (Warszawa, 1895), pp. 9–12.

60 *Diariusz kampanii smoleńskiej Władysława IV 1633–1634*, Mirosław Nagielski (ed.) (Warszawa, 2006), p. 112.

Butler's troops, initially one regiment of infantry and one of dragoons, later his own foot guard regiment. They managed to break through to Butler's position and relieve his hard-pressed soldiers. While heavy fighting continued for the next week, on the night of 27–28 September the Polish regiments finally established a passage to Smoleńsk – the relief was successful. On 4 October the Muscovites withdrew their forces from their positions around Smoleńsk, abandoning all camps on the western side of the city and gathering their troops in the main army camp. The further stages of the campaign, where the Polish–Lithuanian army surrounded the Muscovite camp and attempted to force Shein to surrender, were full of bloody assaults, where infantry from both armies often ended up in bitter hand-to-hand combat. On 19 October Butler's troops took part in fighting for the Żaworonkowe Hills (*Żaworonkowe Wzgórza*), as part of Hetman Radziwiłł's division. Both sides took heavy losses that day, during the fight 'infantry colonel Butler was shot',[61] but the Muscovites were gradually pushed back from their positions. As one of the eyewitness wrote after the October fights, 'shooting here was so intense that all old soldiers that fought in the battles in Livonia, Prussia and in Muscovy admit that they had never before been under such fire.'[62] Butler's regiments were again in action on 17 November, clashing with Muscovite soldiers attempting to build a sconce in front of the Polish troops. For the next few months Władysław IV's army focused on blocking the Muscovite camp, sending cavalry raids to harass supply convoys and prevent any reinforcements to reach Shein. When on 7 January 1634 the Muscovite army attempted to break through Polish lines, again it was Butler that became hero of the hour, as just prior to Shein's attack, the Irishman led both his regiments to set up an ambush on the Muscovites. Thanks to such fortunate coincidence, his soldiers were able to stop approaching the enemy and raise the general alarm in their own camp. The Muscovite attack was repulsed and Shein decided to wait for a relief force sent by the Tsar. In the meantime both sides focused on negotiations and Butler was included in a group of Polish negotiators. Once Shein realised that there was no chance for help from other Muscovite troops, he decided to surrender his army. An act of capitulation was agreed on 24 February 1634, and one of the six Polish commissars signing it was 'Jakub Butler, Royal Courtier and Colonel of His Royal Highness.'[63]

While we lack more detailed information about his service, Murray seems to retain royal favour and in autumn 1633 received a commission to raise a regiment of foot. It is a very interesting document and we are lucky indeed to have it available in English.[64] Murray, with his loose approach to foreign names – rather typical, for Polish documents of that period – is called Mori and Mory, titled Colonel and, besides the new commission, has his command over 200 royal dragoons confirmed.[65]

61 Jan Moskorzowski, *Dyariusz…*, op. cit., p. 47

62 *Ibid.*, p. 58.

63 *Diariusz kampanii smoleńskiej…*, op. cit., p. 289.

64 *Papers relating to the Scots in Poland 1576–1798*, Archibald Francis Steuart (ed.) (Edinburgh, 1915), pp. 10–11.

65 Such dual command was very common, as we can see in the case of Butler during the same war.

Copy of His Royal Majesty's Letters on behalf of Colonel James Mori, given to him for the raising of Infantry. Done in the Castle of Cracow.

Vladislas the Fourth, by the Grace of God King of Poland, Grand Duke of Lithuania, Russia, Prussia, Zmudzia, Masovia, and Inflantia; Hereditary King of the Swedes, Goths, and Vandals; Elected Grand Tsar of Muscovy.

To the Noble James Mory, our faithful Colonel, welcome to us by our grace, noble, faithful, and agreeable, being much recommended to us by our Counsellors and Courtiers for his knightly valour and victories in the present Muscovite expedition.

We and the Republic have been witnesses of your bravery under the walls of Smolensk during the whole time of the siege, so that we not only gave our approval of your command over 200 Dragoons by our private letter, but have chosen you as our Colonel, so that, in addition to the above-mentioned 200 Dragoons, you may collect, by virtue of this present letter, Eight Hundred Foot of foreigners. Over these, for Captains you shall have the Noble Abraham Zalko, Jacob Heykin, Hedda Hernek, and Thomas Lipin, whose energy, courage, and daring are well known to us. They shall be under your command, so that you may present yourself at Smolensk by the first day of the month of June in the year 1634. By which time the Well-born Alexander Korvin Gosiewski, Vojewoda of Smolensk, as Field-Scrivener of the Grand Duchy of Lithuania, shall summon these foot-men together and also make a list of those 200 Dragoons. According to your old list and according as you sign shall our Treasury pay them, that is, inasmuch as you shall draw up new Cavalry. The pay of the foreign soldiers shall be according to that of other Infantry. Pay ought to be in three months' time, and if the Treasury can pay quicker, then you must show your accounts every month. And if their number does not reach the sum mentioned, the amount they would be paid shall be defaulted to the Colonel—the amount to be paid to the wounded and those who have died. If likewise, the Colonel or Captains gave to a wounded soldier or to one who has since died, for his needs, then this sum, upon his showing proofs, shall be rewarded to him. We likewise allow you for your rations as to other Colonels, by the month, for every squadron, at the rate of 100 zloty. The Infantry must give us and the Republic the ordinary oath, and at times dig trenches and help the Polish army to make earthworks. If, also, one of the officers of foot were wounded or bulleted then he must be cured and set free from looking after his work. If, after the formation of this regiment, it happened they were not needed, we shall have a mind for their costs and trouble. This also we add, that you, sir, and your regiment shall be under the command and jurisdiction of the Well-born Wojewoda of Smolensk, who has our confidence.

This our letter we sign with our own hand, and set thereto the Seal of the Grand Duchy of Lithuania.

Given in copy at Smolensk on the 19th day of October1633.—Castr. Crac, t. 58, f. 249.

While we cannot confirm how long it took him to raise this new unit and what strength the regiment reached at the end, we can definitely find evidence of its battle record. On 26 February 1634 Murray is mentioned, leading a 'banner of infantry' as part of the force that was taking control of *Virgin Hill* (*Dziewicze Wzgórze*) from the surrendering Muscovites.[66] Between March and April 1634, Murray's unit was taking part in a siege of the small fortress of Biała. Sadly, this was due to be final episode in the Scot's military career in Poland. At dawn of 6 April, the Muscovites surprised the Polish troops, striking at the position held by Jakub Weyher's and Murray's foot regiments.The Poles were caught completely off guard and the Muscovite foray managed to capture eight standards: four from Weyher's and four from Murray's regiment.[67] Even the colonels took some personal losses, when attackers pillaged their tents – Murray lost his sword and Weyher his coat lined with lynx fur. While losses amongst the troops were very low (one killed, a few wounded and three captured Poles), it was a huge blow to the Polish army's morale. The High Command's reaction was immediate and the next day a martial court was set up to deal with the issue. The investigation pointed out that the blame for such disaster lay totally on Murray's shoulders. As one of the participants of the campaign wrote in his diary:

> Colonel More [Murray] didn't prepare proper defences for his position (as there were only few men on guard, while there should be 30) and he did not check his guards, and his captain, who should be in charge, was [instead] having dinner with colonel [Murray] while the Muscovites attacked. Therefore, with full agreement of all colonels [both national and foreign troops] and by decree of the hetman, his colonelcy is taken away and he is discharged from the army. [His] captain, ensign and sergeant are sentenced to death, as the attack occurred when they were in charge.[68]

Murray was discharged without a pay and his regiment was disbanded, with his troops most likely dispersed between other regiments. We cannot find further information about him but in Poznań (Posen) in 1649 there was a citizen called Jacobus Mora, which is a Latinised version of Murray's name. While it could be coincidence, it is still possible that the disgraced officer settled in Poland, however we do not have hard evidence of it.

In March 1635, during another Polish *Sejm*, it was agreed that Butler would finally be paid back 25,000 zlotys, to cover expenses for raising and equipping his regiment fighting in Prussia in 1628 and 1629.[69] Sadly I have not able to find information about when (or if!) the Crown Treasury did in fact paid him back this money. The Smoleńsk War was not the last campaign in Butler's career. In summer 1635 we see him again as a 'Royal colonel', leading an infantry regiment of 600 men and a small unit of dragoons against the Swedes. A powerful military demonstration led by King Władysław IV was enough to convince the Swedes, at that time hard pressed in Germany, to negotiate for peace. On 12 September 1635 both sides signed a 26.5–year truce in Sztumska

66 Jan Moskorzowski, *Dyariusz…*, op. cit., p. 107.

67 Most likely indicates all standards from each regiment.

68 Jan Moskorzowski, *Dyariusz…*, op. cit., pp. 124–125.

69 *Volumina Legum*, volume III (Petersburg, 1859), p. 414.

Wieś (Stuhmsdorf), one that led to the ceasing of Polish–Swedish hostilities until 1655. Butler's units were, like the majority of the Polish army, disbanded in December 1635. He seems to have abandoned military service at that point and probably settled in Poland. Some secondary sources mentioned his name again in 1652, as one of the Polish officers killed by Tatars and Cossacks after the battle of Batoh, but it seems that they confused him with one of the other Butlers, probably from the Courland-based line of the family. In 1641 one Jacob Butler, named as Royal courtier, purchased some land near town Częstochowa.[70] Unfortunately it is impossible to confirm if it was the former colonel or some other Butler, again from the Courland or Prussian line.

The careers of Aston, Butler and Murray in Polish service are just a small sample of the rich history of British mercenaries serving in the 17th century in the Polish–Lithuanian Commonwealth. They fought for Sigismund III and Władysław IV in a turbulent period, when the country was often engaged in two conflicts at the same time. They served with distinction, drawing praise and favour from their commanders. Amongst many other foreigners, they helped introduce a Western style of modern warfare into the Commonwealth's armies, which was successfully merged with the already well established Eastern style.

70 Adam Boniecki, *Herbarz polski*, volume II (Warszawa, 1900), p. 263.

3

Establishing Control: Creating the High Commands in 1642[1]

Professor Martyn Bennett

Introduction

Over 170 men and one woman at the very least served in general officer rank served in one or more of the armies raised in Britain and Ireland put into the field between 1639 and 1660. They had very different backgrounds, had a varying degree of military and other experiences, differing educational backgrounds before the war. They were to hold very different roles and experienced victory and defeat, and it is true that whilst a few of them reached the heights of national celebrity during the wars and historical fame thereafter, some disappeared into the deepest obscurity that a person who once held a rank of such potential could do. These generals were appointed to a great variety of tasks and responsibilities and this paper covers only a tiny number of them – those appointed to lead the King's and Parliament's forces during the year 1642 and the very start of 1643. As such it is just the beginning of an attempt to study them all to a greater or lesser degree. Those discussed today fall broadly into two camps: field army generals and the earliest appointments to regional management roles.

This is an early public outing for material from a research project – Cromwell's Rivals – which intends to analyse the leadership capabilities of the general officers of the Civil Wars. This project examines the people who were appointed or promoted to the rank of general, that is to say colonel general, during the wars from 1638–1660. It will be a prosopographical study aimed partly at why these men acted as they did in terms of their wartime experience set against their pre-Civil War background. It hope to be able to define why generals were generals and why they were successful

1 An earlier version of this paper was given at the Friends of the National Civil War Centre and Battlefields Trust Conference on 12 May 2018, and this revised version was presented to the Helion, Century of the Soldier: England Turned Germany Conference on 22 May 2018. I am grateful for all the comments and suggestions made by the delegates at both conferences.

or unsuccessful. The project will explore such questions as how much of their career development depended on social and political status, particularly, but not exclusively, in its early stages, and how much depended on demonstrable skill and experience. The project will also consider Napoleon's question asked of a suitably qualified colonel proposed for general officer rank: is he lucky? My first task has been to compile a list of all the generals in the period, currently that list stands at 171.[2] That is 170-plus men and one women – Queen Henrietta Maria.

In 1642, following two wars between Scotland the rest of Charles I's kingdoms, a rebellion and war in Ireland, England and Wales collapsed into armed conflict. Having failed to defeat a Scottish rebellion and having been implicated in the rebellion in Ireland by one of its leaders, Charles I tried to seize the political initiative. However his attempted *coup d'etat* failed, and in its wake Parliament took control of the county trained band leadership. This essay discusses, against the backdrop of a descent into war, attempts by both sides to create command structures for their rival armed forces.

This chapter will focus on the beginnings of the Civil War in England and Wales: however, it must be remembered that two wars had already been fought to a conclusion within the British Isles and that in 1642 there was a suite of general officers in Scotland and serving in Ireland too. Therefore although there were at least 36 men who seem to have held general rank in as war broke out in England, six of them were generals fighting in Ireland during that year, therefore they do not fall into the focus of this paper, which will concentrate on the generals who took part in the early campaigns in England and Wales.

The Militia Ordinance

The Irish rebellion of 22 October 1641 began whilst King Charles I was in Edinburgh ostensibly to sign the peace treaty ending the state of war between his Scottish kingdom and his other realms. Charles had hoped to forge a 'Royalist' party in order to overthrow the dominant covenanter group led by the Earl of Argyll. The plot had been exposed by one of the future Civil War generals Sir John Hurry (or Urry), but such was the terror inspired by the rebellion, that both sides sought to cover up the plot in order to present a show of unity. The Westminster parliament continued this 'policy' by ensuring that the King was welcomed home to London. The business of both the estates and Parliament was to create an expeditionary force to send to Ireland and establish the financial support necessary to do so.

The King, not surprisingly, assumed that he would command the forces raised for the campaign in Ireland, either in person or in proxy through a lord or captain general chosen by him. There were, however a number of difficulties preventing this from happening. Creating the army command during the two Scottish or Bishops' Wars in 1639 and 1640 should have been straightforward. Whilst the great strategic plan had involved Sir Thomas Wentworth, Lord Deputy of Ireland, was to raise an army in Ireland

2 This is the case in June 2019.

intended for a campaign on the west coast of Scotland: the Marquess of Hamilton was similarly charged with raising an amphibious forces for a descent on Scotland's east coast. However, the plan was never fully developed and only the English and Welsh forces – the Trained Bands or militia – were dispatched to the Scottish borders by the land route. In the first war the army was led by a lord general, Thomas Howard, Earl of Arundel, a man of no discernible military experience, seconded by Henry Rich Earl of Holland – the Queen's choice – who had some military experience gained in the 1610s and had been captain of the yeomen of the guard, notable military experience as lieutenant general.[3] It may be possible that he was seconded by Viscount Conway, a man with some Continental experience as a military command.[4] At this point an issue arose which was to raise its head several times over the next decade. The King demonstrated a good deal of personal indecisiveness and perhaps confusion during the period, and this led to his rapid changeability which had consequences for army command: he was also susceptible to taking the Queen's advice, regardless of its merit. This was quickly manifest: an obvious choice for command in some eyes was Robert Devereux, Earl of Essex who had recent experience abroad, but he was initially passed over possibly due to the Queen's intervention, and then somewhat tardily given the rank of lieutenant generalship of the foot and made second in command to Arundel. That this was an afterthought is underlined by the fact that this was an unusual arrangement because the commander of the foot was usually accorded the rank of sergeant-major general and the position of second in command was usually the lieutenant general of horse – which would have been in this case the Earl of Holland who had been appointed at the outset. Essex was by far the most experienced of the high commanders. None of his colleagues in the King's forces had much of an opportunity to shine or add substantially to their personal credit during the first Bishops' War, but worse was to come.

In the second Bishops' War the King changed the command structure: Arundel, Essex, and Holland were set aside, much to their chagrin, and according to Edward Hyde, later Earl of Clarendon, driven into the arms of the King's opponents.[5] Algernon Percy, Earl of Northumberland, was appointed lord general: he was a man with no experience of land war service, but had – possibly because of the Queen's intervention – succeeded the Earl of Lindsey as admiral of the so-called 'ship-money fleet' and set about attacking Dutch fishing boats. Northumberland was an ally of Sir Thomas Wentworth, and was thus probably both a political and magnate appointment. The Percys were incredibly potent in the north-east of England where the King expected to launch his campaign. But there followed a bout of his recurring illness, which may have been political, although Clarendon said it was a serious bout.[6] The King appointed

3 Bulstrode Whitelocke, *Memorials of the English Affairs during the reign of King Charles I*, four volumes (Oxford, 1853), Vol 1, pp.86–87.

4 *Oxford Dictionary of National Biography* [*ODNB*], Edward Conway Viscount Conway.

5 Clarendon, *History of the Rebellion and Civil Wars in England*, (Oxford,1992 originally 1888, edited by W. Dunn Macray), vol. I, p.185

6 Clarendon, vol. I, p.189

Sir Thomas Wentworth, now elevated to the title Earl of Strafford and already captain-general of the Irish army, as a replacement commander, albeit with the title of lieutenant general in deference to Northumberland's earlier commission.[7] This appointment was again questionable as Wentworth, despite his position as commander in chief in Ireland, had no military experience at all. However, Wentworth too was ill and real command in the field fell upon the shoulders of the lieutenant general, Edward, 2nd Viscount Conway, a man who was nephew to Horace Vere, and had served in his uncle's garrison at Brill and was to be found holding a command in many actions 'of the English at sea or land'.[8] Conway held the post of 'general of horse' having been the first of the commanders at the border, and was now thrust into the position of command to face the Scottish onslaught.[9] After the defeat at Newburn, Clarendon said caustically of him that he was 'never after turning his face towards the enemy, or doing anything like a commander'; Bulstrode Whitelocke likewise commented that Conway's actions being examined; 'he used his best art and flourishes to vindicate himself, yet something stuck upon him'.[10] Below the level of the confused high command, the collective record of experience was stronger. Henry Wilmot was an experienced veteran of the wars on the Continent starting as captain of horse in Dutch service who had been wounded at Breda in 1637. He was Conway's commissary general of the horse.[11] Sir Jacob Astley was Major General in command of the foot. Astley was an experienced soldier, whose war record stretched back to the Azores in the 1590s and included service with the Dutch and Swedish forces in the intervening years. Astley had the dual advantage of military experience and political connections as we shall see later, the King was, of course, overall commander. Even so it was not able to withstand the successful campaign mounted by Alexander Leven, who defeated the King's army at the Battle of Newburn and then occupied the north of England.

However, in February 1642, in the wake of the Irish Rebellion, the issue of command was different. Several of the Irish rebels has asserted that the King and Queen were in sympathy with their cause. Even more alarmingly Sir Phelim O'Neill had declared that he had a commission from the King authorising the rebellion.[12] There was thus, an atmosphere of mistrust at the highest level which was coupled with knowledge of the Queen's purpose in going abroad following the King's catastrophic blunder in attempting to charge five MPs and one member of the House of Lords with treason in January 1642. Charles was, therefore, considered unsuitable for command. Nevertheless, the monarch was still the fountain of military command in the country: the only person who could legally appoint the commanders of the Trained Bands the county-based lord

7 Whitelocke, vol. l, p.101.

8 Clarendon, vol. I, p.186.

9 Whitelocke, vol. I, p.102.

10 Clarendon, vol. I, pp.189, 190; Whitelocke, vol. I, p.103.

11 Clarendon, vol. I, p.206; Whitelocke, vol. I, pp.102–103.

12 Corish, Patrick, 'The Rising of 1641 and the Catholic Confederacy', in Moody, F.X. Martin and F.J. Byrne, *A New History of Ireland* (Oxford: Oxford University Press, 1976), vol. 3, pp.291–293.

lieutenants. This was not a power he would relinquish willingly. Parliament wanted to take control of the county trained bands, at this point, at least temporarily, but attempts to persuade the King to acquiesce failed, forcing Parliament to take radical action. A militia bill was drafted with the aim of reorganising the lieutenancy by recalling all existing lieutenancy commissions and issuing new ones. This Parliament hoped would weed out papists and enthusiastic supporters of the King. The King could not accept this and refused to accede to the bill. Parliament eventually circumvented him and issued the bill as an ordinance, partly using the claim that the King was absent from Westminster (he was by now on his way to York).[13] An ordinance was an executive tool used when the monarch was absent from the seat of government, abroad or physically or mentally ill. In 'normal' circumstances the ordinance would be signed by the monarch later when returned to full health and/or the capital. It was clear to many that at this point in time only force of arms could gain this King's assent. There was little talk of compromise on the ordinance: the MPs forwarded the names of proposed new lieutenants and on 5 March the ordinance was passed and plans for defending the great ports of Hull and Portsmouth were put in place.[14]

Proxy Generals: the Lord Lieutenants

It was some time before the ordinance was put fully into action. Some sitting lord lieutenants only reluctantly handed in their commissions and some new appointees were equally reluctant to collect theirs. Buckinghamshire's Lord Paget took up his appointment, only to leave the office in June.[15] Likewise, the lieutenants were not always assiduous in their duties. Only 14 English counties held musters under the new legislation in the early summer. In those conforming counties some men stand out: in Lincolnshire Lord Willoughby of Parham and Warwickshire's Lord Brooke were enthusiasts and both would later hold general officer commands in the forthcoming war. In other places different men had to step into the official lieutenant's shoes: thoroughgoing oppositionist Parliamentarian Lord Saye and Sele took charge of Gloucestershire after the original appointee Lord Chandos showed himself as a supporter of the King.[16] Sir William Brereton MP took charge of Cheshire and he like Brooke and Willoughby would become a general officer in the war.[17] These men who did take up Parliament's commission would be the first of the Civil War commanders, in charge of the nearest thing England and Wales had to a standing army, the county

13 Clarendon, vol. II, p.1.

14 Gardiner, S.R. (ed.), *Constitutional Documents of the Puritan Revolution* (Oxford: Oxford University Press, 1978), pp.245–247.

15 Northamptonshire County Record Office, Finch Hatton Manuscripts 133, Buckinghamshire entry for the Militia Ordinance, np.

16 Whitelocke, *Memorials*, vol.I, pp.182–183.

17 The original appointee to command there was James, Lord Strange, soon to be the Earl of Derby: Brereton had been appointed to original committee and also to several of the sub-committees; Finch Hatton, entry for the Cheshire County Committees, np.

militia known as the trained bands. The lieutenancy role would be emulated later in the war by officially appointed county-level generals, posts which some of the lieutenants went on to fill, but for the time being these men were proxy generals.

The Royalist Response

Eventually, having failed to reach a compromise on the militia proposals the King made his move.[18] In May 1642 Charles, having also failed to stop the Militia Ordinance from being put into practice, issued commissions of array to selected county gentlemen and nobles requiring them to meet as a military 'committee' similar to a commission of the peace.[19] The commission of array had a long-standing historical precedent and predated the office of lord lieutenant. The issue of the commissions was similar in intent to the Militia Ordinance, in that like the ordinance, firstly it enjoined the appointees to raise the trained bands in their counties and secondly, it too was only put into effect in a few counties: just 11 held musters under the commissions of array, 10 in England and one in Wales, although this latter was Monmouth, administratively part of England since the 1540s.[20] Even so, there were enthusiasts: Lord Mohun was very active in Cornwall and in Monmouthshire the powerful Somerset family led by the Earl of Worcester took charge. His son, Lord Herbert, seized the county magazine and raised the shire militia after the war had begun. In Leicestershire and Rutland the Militia Ordinance had displaced the joint lord lieutenants, the head of the Hastings family Henry, Earl of Huntingdon, and his son Ferdinando, Lord Hastings. Lord Hastings was sticking with Parliament and the Earl did not seem to resent actively his being supplanted by the Henry Grey, Earl of Stamford.[21] However, Huntingdon's younger son Henry was not so quiescent. He challenged Stamford actively and raised the trained bands in June 1642. Henry Hastings would become a general officer in 1643. His principal opponents, Stamford and his son Thomas, Lord Grey of Groby, would be generals by the end of the year.[22]

Summer 1642 – the Commands Expand

The new lord lieutenants were collectively unable to bring together the trained bands in the numbers Parliament required; fortunately for them, neither were their opponents. The trained bands therefore formed a generally insignificant role in army creation, with the exception of the London regiments, which were to provide useful reinforcements for the Parliamentarian armies in the south and west during the next three years. This cadre of early appointments already contained a collection of

18 Clarendon, vol. II, p.42.

19 Gardiner, *Constitutional Documents*, pp.258–261.

20 Fletcher, A., *The Outbreak of the English Civil War* (London: Edward Arnold, 1981), p.285.

21 Finch Hatton Manuscripts 133, entries under Leicestershire for the Militia Ordinance and the Commission of Array, np.

22 Historical Manuscripts Commission, Report on the Manuscripts of the late Reginald Rawdon Hastings, (London 1930), vol. II, p.94.

varied men in various types of roles before the end of 1642, with different roles and responsibilities. Of this number, seven of the Royalist generals were commanders who played a role in the first campaign of the war, which stretched from September to late November 1642. They were members of the King's field army assembled in the late summer which had marched from Nottingham to Shrewsbury and down into the south Midlands where it fought the Battle of Edgehill on 23 October 1642, before advancing on London. It was not to have a harmonious leadership, as there were conflicting authorities which arose from both the appointments process and prickly personalities. Charles I was in the field with this army and therefore his presence as overall commander was potentially a cause of friction and confusion.

Unlike as had been the case with the first and second of the Bishops' Wars, the King did not create a command structure solely from political appointees for the field army, although the picture was different with the later regional commands. There were no inexperienced or 'wing-chair generals': instead there was, on paper at least, a solid cadre of veterans. At its head was Robert Bertie, the 60-year-old Earl of Lindsey, who was given the rank of lord general the commander in chief until the Battle of Edgehill.[23] Lindsey had service on the Continent possibly dating back to the 1590s and was part of the Vere family circle: indeed his first verifiable military role was at the Battle of Nieuwpoort in 1600 under Sir Francis Vere. But despite military connections to the current Earl of Essex's father – who was his godfather – the King of Denmark, through a short-lived commission in 1612–14, and Prince Maurice in the failed attempt to break the siege of Breda in 1624, his military record was not as strong as that of Patrick Ruthven of whom more later.[24] From the mid 1620s Lindsey had held naval commands both before and after the assassination of Buckingham, but, whilst in these he was generally unsuccessful, he had escaped with his reputation intact. From 1635–37 he was admiral of the newly created fleet – the 'ship-money fleet' – before being passed over in favour of the Earl of Northumberland for command of this fleet and the title Lord High Admiral. After the 1620s, his experience of armies was limited to being firstly a deputy and later the lord lieutenant of Lincolnshire. He was also a privy councillor from 1628 when he had first become a member of the King's council of war.[25]

Lindsey was a fairly reluctant Royalist in many ways, despite being restored by the King to the office of lord lieutenant of Lincolnshire in defiance of the Militia Ordinance, and head of the county's commission of array from early summer 1640. He nevertheless was given command of the King's proto-field army.[26] However Lindsey did not enjoy the role fully for long, for he was superseded – unofficially at first – by

23 Bulstrode Whitelocke suggests that Edward Seymour, Marquess of Hertford was the initial choice. Whitelocke, *Memorials of the English Affairs* (Oxford: Oxford University Press, 1853), vol. I, p.181.

24 Peter Young, *Edgehill, 1642: the Campaign and the Battle* (Kineton: Roundwood Press, 1967), p.61.

25 *ODNB*, entry for Robert Bertie, Earl of Lindsey.

26 Finch Hatton, 133, entries under Lincolnshire, np.

the King's nephew Prince Rupert, second son of Charles's sister Elizabeth and the Elector Palatine Frederick, the short-lived queen and king of Bohemia. Aged just 23 in 1642, Rupert joined the King during the summer and despite his inexperience was given the title general of horse in August 1642 – a clear conflict of roles as Lindsey was apparently not consulted and this effectively made Rupert second in command; but worse than that he was exempted from Lindsey's command and could only be given orders by the King.[27] Rupert had fought in the Continental wars but had spent a great deal of time in honourable, if sometimes very close, captivity after being taken prisoner at the Battle of Eiburg in 1637.[28] Lindsey must have felt naturally disenchanted with this clear trespass on his responsibilities.[29] Therefore, before the campaign got underway fully there was already a conflict within the command structure with two members of the royal family, the King and Rupert holding positions which would allow them to supersede their commissioned generals like Lindsey.[30]

Patrick Ruthven, Lord Forth, who had served the King in 1639 and 1640, was appointed marshal general of the army, with responsibility for deploying the army on a battlefield. This was an informed choice: some the veterans of the King's armies in the wars against Scotland, including the earls of Essex and Northumberland, were firmly in the Parliamentarian camp, and Essex was to become Parliament's lord general. Ruthven was 69 years old, born in Ballindean, the second son of William Ruthven and Katherine Stewart. He had served in foreign armies in Europe from 1608 onwards, and then most notably in Gustavus Adolphus's Polish campaign during the 1620s. He was knighted by the Swedish king after the Battle of Dirschau and appointed governor of Ulm in Bavaria in 1632, rising through the ranks of major general to lieutenant general by the mid 1630s; he was present at the Battle of Breitenfeld in 1631. In the Bishops' Wars he served the King in Edinburgh; he was appointed governor of the castle in 1639 and 1640, but was only able to make his mark in the second Bishops' War when he held out in the castle until mid September 1640, after the Battle of Newburn had effectively ended the war.[31] Nevertheless it was recognised that the position of a marshal was potentially the cause of a rift and/or rivalry in command. John Cruso even suggested that whilst the lord general was away from the army he take either the marshal or the lieutenant general of horse with him to prevent rivalries developing between the two in his absence.[32] What was worse was that Clarendon believed that Ruthven was always with the horse before Edgehill, thus pushing Henry Wilmot further out of the picture.[33]

27 Clarendon, vol. II, p.350.

28 Kitson, F., *Prince Rupert, Portrait of a Soldier* (London: Constable, 1994), pp.67–68, 84–85.

29 Clarendon, vol. II, pp.350–351.

30 Clarendon, vol. II, p.366.

31 *ODNB*, entry for Patrick Ruthven, Earl of Forth; Peter Newman, *Royalist officers in England and Wales, 1642–1660* (New York: Garland, 1981), p.187, no. 713.

32 Cruso, John, *Military Instructions for the Cavalry* (Cambridge, 1632), p.4.

33 Clarendon, vol. II, p.348.

Command of the foot was given to Sir Jacob Astley, with as customarily the case, the rank of major general. Astley was undoubted experienced. He too had been militarily active in the 1590s, fighting alongside both Sir Walter Raleigh and the Earl of Essex; in the following decade he served with Sir Henry Vere and may well have been at the Battle of Nieuwpoort like Lindsey. He went on to serve with Palatinate, Danish and Swedish forces through the 1610s, 20s and 30s and sometime tutored the very young Prince Rupert. In the Bishops' Wars he had already served in the role of major general. By the time of the Bishops' Wars, Astley had acquired the reputation of being an experienced commander of foot and an acknowledged military administrator.[34] His silence in October 1642 did nothing to ease the problems of command.

In charge of the supplying of the army was 33-year-old Commissary General Henry Wilmot. Wilmot, third son of Viscount Wilmot, had sat as an MP in the 1620s and had then served in the Dutch army during the 1630s and been wounded at the siege of Breda in 1637. Wilmot had also served in the post of commissary general during the Bishops' Wars, being captured at the Battle of Newburn in August 1640, before returning to a seat in the Long Parliament for Tamworth; he had been involved in the Army Plot of 1641 and was in favour with the Queen at the time, although he was disliked by Prince Rupert. In 1642, Wilmot might have been considered for command of the horse, but the lieutenant generalcy was left vacant when Rupert was appointed 'general of horse'.[35] Instead, although in mid summer he led the King's Horse he only held the rank of commissary general.[36] The dragoons were led by Sir Arthur Aston, another veteran with the rank of colonel general.[37] Aston was the at least 49 years old son of a soldier in whose regiment he had served as a captain and later lieutenant colonel. He fought in the Russian and Polish armies and was present at the Battle of Lützen as a colonel.[38] He served in several general officer commands in the Bishops' Wars, and would be promoted again by the end of the year.[39]

It is true to say that this was an experienced high command, but it had met with mixed success during the months in which the army was brought together: Rupert, Wilmot and Lindsey were the least experienced in most recent European wars, although Rupert had used his long captivity to study the recent developments in land warfare.[40] The King was the one without any real military experience and had been conspicuously less martial than his elder brother, Henry Prince of Wales, who had died in 1612.[41] The varying levels and types of experience proved not to put the Royalist army at a disadvantage in the early stages of the war; it is true to say that both sides

34 *ODNB*, entry for Jacob Lord Astley; Newman, *Royalist Officers*, pp.9–10, no. 39.

35 *ODNB*, entry under Henry Lord Wilmot.

36 Clarendon, vol. II, p.288.

37 Clarendon, vol. II, p.348.

38 *ODNB*, entry for Sir Arthur Aston.

39 Bodleian Library, *Black: Docquets of Letters Patent*, f.4.

40 Kitson, *Prince Rupert*, p.68.

41 Strong, Roy, *Henry, Prince of Wales* (London: Thames and Hudson, 1986), pp.45–48.

were groping their way to the required levels of professionalism in 1642. Rather it was the clash of roles and personalities which lay at the core of the important disputes in the early days. Coupled with the King's (changeable) selection of favourites, which would remain an issue throughout the war, the clash of personalities would hamper the development of unity at the highest level and lead to the death of the Earl of Lindsey. The King had gradually begun to ignore Lindsey following the raising of the standard on 22 August at Nottingham, allowing the young Prince Rupert to lead the horse in independent actions around the Midlands. Thus it was Rupert who led the horse in the field and began to gain a reputation, which was until Powick Bridge untested. He was also capable of gross errors, which it is likely that experienced county governor Lindsey would not make, such as demanding £2,000 from the town of Leicester on 6 September 1642: a sum which was equivalent to almost 60 percent of the county's annual ship money levies and which no doubt left the town more willing to adopt Parliamentarian leadership in the months which followed.[42]

The management crisis, according to legend, came at the worst possible moment: on 23 October 1642, as the King's army was being marshalled into battle formation just below Edgehill, near Kineton in Warwickshire, although Professor Wanklyn is rightly sceptical and suggests that it is likely that it was a council of war debate, far from the battlefield. Indeed the Earl of Clarendon implies that it was on 22 October at the latest.[43] The commanders began to argue about the battle formation. All of them with the exception of the King had been involved, to a greater or lesser extent, in the wars on the Continent, where different formations for individual foot regiments and horse regiments were brought together with changes in the way whole armies were being drawn up for battle. The pace of change was relatively quick, but even if it had not been, the experience time-span was in some cases 50 years in duration. The most recent war on the Continent, that which would become known as the Thirty Years' War, had seen a relatively quick turnover of ideas. The King's generals had experienced these changes, but chiefly from the perspective of the army they fought with. Prince Rupert had studied the warfare techniques brought into the conflict by the Swedish king, Gustavus Adolphus, and both Ruthven and Astley had actually fought with the King's army. Naturally they might be expected to wish to follow the techniques they had experienced and learned. Lindsey however remained attached to Dutch formations he had seen developed by the Dutch military tactician, Prince Maurice, earlier in the century. On that October day, both battlefield strategies had their merits. The newer tactics learned by Rupert largely theoretically, and by Ruthven in the field during service with the Swedes, were certainly more modern. Lindsey may have been right: the Dutch

42 *A true relation of Prince Robert's Proceedings in Leicestershire* (London, 1642), passim; Nichols, J. (ed.), *The History and Antiquities of the County of Leicester* (Leicester, 1804), vol. III, part II, appendix 4. Pp.30, 31; Stocks, Helen (ed.), *Records of the Borough of Leicester* (Cambridge: Cambridge Univeresity Press, 1923), pp.317–319.

43 Clarendon, vol.II, p.367.

tactics were probably better understood in Britain and thus required less experience on behalf of the undertrained army.[44] However, Ruthven's promotion of the Swedish tactics also made sense as it would have provided some compensation for the lack of muskets in the Royalist foot regiments.[45] However, the Earl was now held in less esteem than the young Rupert who had already won a famous, if small scale, victory at Powick Bridge on 23 September 1642.[46] Ruthven and the Prince were quietly backed by Astley who as major general should have had an important role in the decision, but was no doubt conscious of his social inferiority in an argument between a prince and earl, and by the fact that he was a favourite of Elizabeth, Queen of Bohemia, a former tutor of the Prince and who personally favoured the tactics of Gustavus Adolphus. Yet it was the support of fellow royal, the King, which swung the decision and thus Rupert's view won through. Lindsey, no doubt already feeling undermined by the newcomer prince handed back his seemingly pointless commission, stormed off and joined his own regiment of foot.[47] He died in action during the day.

Essex's Boys

There was much less confusion in Parliament's high command, but the leadership structure was not to be a finished product before Edgehill. Robert Devereux, the 51-year-old 3rd Earl of Essex, was the heir of Essex the rebel and doomed favourite of Elizabeth I. Essex's bleak marital and sex life left him open to Royalist jokes throughout the war. He had experience of the wars in northern Europe. He had been snubbed by the Queen in 1640 when Arundel had been give command of the army Essex thought he deserved and which he may well have been lined up for, were it not for her interference. Essex had been a colonel of a foot regiment as early as 1624, he also had given long service as the lord lieutenant of Shropshire.[48] It was Essex who had been belatedly appointed to the position of lieutenant general in the first Bishops' War and ignored when the second army was drawn up a year later. Despite being restored to his father's attainted titles by King James, Essex, perhaps partly because of the shoddy way he had been treated in 1639 and 1640, had little compunction in accepting Parliament's offer of the lord generalship.[49]

Essex's general of horse was William Russell, the 26-year-old Earl of Bedford who had no military experience and only succeeded his active oppositionist father

44 Young, *Edgehill*, p.79.
45 Clarendon, vol.II, p.347.
46 *The Latest Remarkable Truths (not before Printed)* (London, 1642), pp.3–4; Clarendon, vol. II, pp.323–326.
47 Clarendon, vol. II, p.358; Malcom Wanklyn, *Warrior Generals: Winning the British Civil Wars* (London: Yale University Press, 2010), p.16.
48 Essex was replaced by Edward Lord Littleton by the Militia Ordinance, but he was given other areas of the country instead: he was lord lieutenant of Yorkshire that year. Northamptonshire Record Office, Finch Hatton 133, entries under Shropshire and Yorkshire, np.
49 ODNB, entry under Robert Devereux, Earl of Essex.

in 1641.[50] Nevertheless, he had been appointed lieutenant general: no doubt due to his status. Fortunately, Bedford was seconded by Sir William Balfour.[51] Balfour was considerably older than Bedford: his father had been a soldier and Balfour himself was a lieutenant in the Scottish brigade in the Netherlands as early as the 1590s. Whilst his early service was in the foot, by 1615 he was in command of harquebusiers.[52] At that time, harquebusiers were a much maligned branch of the horse, considered by some as a form of dragoons. However, by the Civil War this experience placed Balfour in a good position for the harquebusier was becoming the chief type of horse troops used in Britain and Ireland and because of the decline in the use of expensive cuirassiers were becoming the heavy cavalry of Europe.[53] Essex's major general was Sir John Meyrick (or Merrick) who was a 42-year-old veteran of the wars in Europe who had fought alongside Essex and worked with the Earl in Shropshire when Essex was lord lieutenant; it had been the Earl's patronage which got Merrick a parliamentary seat for Newcastle-under-Lyme.[54] The two remaining Parliamentarian generals were the 43-year-old John Mordaunt, Earl of Peterborough, who commanded Essex's ordnance, and Sir James Ramsay the commissary general.[55] Peterborough had only domestic peacetime experience as a deputy lieutenant, and latterly the new lord lieutenant in Northamptonshire. He was seconded by Lieutenant Philibert Emanuel de Boyes.[56] Ramsey was a different kettle of fish, having served in Swedish forces during the 1530s. He had been listed as a captain in Essex's own regiment of horse commanded by Sir Philip Stapleton before being given the commissary general role.[57] There were no arguments in Essex's camp during the drawing up of his army near Kineton. Interestingly Essex's forces did try to use the Swedish method which caused debate in the opposite camp.[58]

Edgehill – the Fortunes of the Generals

On 23 October 1642, the King's army with its latently riven command, marched from its commanding position down Edgehill and advanced upon the Earl of Essex's forces, which were drawn up in a defensive stance in the vale below. The dragoons which Essex had placed on his eastern flank were driven from their positions by their Royalist

50 Clarendon, vol. II, pp.354–35; *ODNB*, entry under William Russell, fifth earl of Bedford; Finch Hatton, 133, entries under Gloucestershire, np.

51 *The list of the Army Raised under the Command of his Excellency, Robert, Earl of Essex* (London, 1642), p.5.

52 Clarendon, vol. II, p.355; *ODNB*, entry under Sir William Balfour.

53 Gaunt, Peter, *The English Civil War a Military History* (London: I.B. Tauris, 2014), p.112.

54 *ODNB*, entry for Sir John Merrick.

55 *ODNB*, entry under John Mordaunt, 5th Earl of Peterborough, and Sir James Ramsey.

56 *The List of the Army*, p.5.

57 Whitelocke, vol. I, p.186. Whitelocke pointed out that Ramsay ('a Scot'), was one of the first to reach Westminster on the day after the Battle of Edgehill claiming that 'the army of parliament was broken'.

58 The Royalists, because of the outcome of the argument between Rupert and Lindsey, had adopted the Swedish tactics for both horse and foot. Keith Roberts, *Pike and Shot Tactics, 1590–1660* (Oxford: Osprey, 2010), p.60.

counterparts, allowing Prince Rupert to lead forward the front line of the Royalist horse on the right flank free from flanking fire. Rupert was in the position on a battlefield which a lieutenant general should occupy: the right of the line. He had, he later claimed, expected the second line to stand in reserve but it followed him in the attack. They were directly opposed by Sir James Ramsay who had decided to use the older Dutch form of horse tactics, which depended upon the firepower of the troopers to break up or disrupt the attack. It did not work: the Prince's men, using Swedish tactics, did not pause to fire their weapons and attacked at some speed, driving Ramsay's men before them, off the field.[59] The second line under Sir John Byron followed Rupert possibly because he initially mistakenly thought that the Parliamentarians were launching a counter-attack. Sir Faithful Fortescue's troop of horse, which changed sides as the attack developed, may just have looked as if it posed a threat because it remained on the field as Ramsay's men fled. Ramsay was barged off the field for about two miles and later had to answer for his conduct at an enquiry in St Albans. Although he was cleared of charges of cowardice, his career may have been damaged.[60] He would only serve as colonel in Essex's army thereafter and would not hold general officer rank until he was appointed major general in the Scottish Army of the Solemn League and Covenant in 1644. Rupert's dramatic success had an enormous effect, convincing one Parliamentarian brigade of foot that the battle was lost, and it collapsed into disorder.

On the western side of the battlefield it was Wilmot the Royalist commissary general who led the Royalist left flank's attack by both lines of horse under his command. Wilmot defeated many of the regiments facing him, but not so comprehensively as Rupert's charge had done. Instead, the failure to completely destroy the Parliamentarian right wing allowed for a counter-attack by Sir William Balfour, which seriously damaged the King's foot regiments in the centre of the battlefield. It was because of Balfour's counter-attack that Essex was able to hold his position on the field and bring the battle to a conclusion through fighting the Royalists to a standstill.

The fortunes of the battlefield generals were therefore mixed on both sides. Rupert and Wilmot came out of the battle rather well and with enhanced reputations, but in reality both had exposed the King and the lord general to great danger and potential defeat. The angry ex-lieutenant general the Earl of Lindsey fought hard in the frontal attack launched by Sir Nicholas Byron on the Earl of Essex's leading (or van) brigade. He was mortally wounded and taken prisoner when the struggle became increasingly furious as Essex's own lifeguard troop joined the fray.[61] On the opposite side fortunes were similarly mixed, Bedford's command largely disappeared from the field, but his

59 See the debate on the speed of an attack by horse in Gavin Robinson, and 'Equine Battering Rams? A Reassessment of Cavalry Charges in the English Civil War', *The Journal of Military History* (75, 3, July 2011), pp.718–732.

60 *ODNB*, entry for Sir James Ramsay.

61 *A Perfect Relation of the Proceedings of Both Armies* (London, 1642), p.5.

deputy, Balfour, met with success, turning the fortunes of the battle; it would not be the last time he saved the face of his commander Essex.[62]

The campaign did not end at Edgehill. Two more battles were fought before the end of that year's campaign. The King's army stopped off in Oxford instead of marching directly on London. This may seem surprising as the Earl of Essex had withdrawn northwards to Warwick initially, leaving London wide open to attack. The King began to create a distant ring around the capital by occupying Oxford, Banbury and Reading. Meanwhile, on the western approach into London, Meyrick, taking advantage of the King's circuitous route, blocked the road. On 12 November the Royalist forces attacked the Parliamentarian forces at Brentford, and by the end of the day had pushed Meyrick back towards Essex's main forces west of the city. On 13 November the King's army came face to face with Essex's army supported by the Major General Philip Skippon, leading the London Trained Bands.[63] This new figure on the stage had extensive military experience. Skippon served with Sir Horace Vere in the Palatinate during the early 1620s and then with Count Mansfeld's forces in the mid 20s. He had fought at both sieges of Breda in 1625 and 1637. He had been recommended by the King to the Honourable Artillery Company in London during the 1630s, but in 1642, after the King's attempt to arrest six members of Parliament, Skippon was given command of the London Trained Bands by Parliament. Turnham Green marked the end of this appointment. Essex secured Skippon's appointment as major general of the field army's foot on 16/17 November 1642. Sir John Meyrick was thereafter given command of the artillery, in the place of the Earl of Peterborough and de Boyes, whose performance in the role was dilatory during the Edgehill campaign. In the Royalist forces, it was Lindsey who was replaced: although he had laid down his commission, he was not replaced until after his death had been confirmed (it was the day after Edgehill). His replacement was Lord Forth.[64]

The Late-1642 Generals

The King backed down at Turnham Green; Essex and Skippon were supported by citizens of London, bringing supplies and appeared on the field armed with makeshift weapons. The Battle of Edgehill had proved that the war would not be concluded by a cataclysmic battle and Turnham Green demonstrated that it would not be a short war.[65] The effect of the realisation that war would continue sparked a second and third wave of appointments to general command on both sides. In many ways these mirrored

62 He would, by escaping through the Royalist lines, extricate Essex's horse from the defeat at the Battle of Lostwithiel on 3 September 1644.

63 Whitelocke, vol. I, pp.190–191.

64 *A True and most succinct relation of the late battell fought near Kinton in Warwickshire* (London, 1642), p.1; *A Full and true relation of the Great Battle fought between the King's Army and his excellency, the Earl of Essex* (London, 1642), p.5; Wanklyn, *Warrior Generals*, p.34.

65 There is a mild suggestion of discord in Essex's camp after Turnham Green when the 'old soldiers of fortune' as Bulstrode Whitelocke called them and on whom Essex relied, advised against pursuing the

what had happened in Ireland during the summer. The Catholic Confederation of Kilkenny came into being during the summer of 1642, which saw the creation of not only a central government and regional administrations, but appointed commanders – generals – in each of the four provinces of Ireland: Thomas Preston for Leinster with the Earl of Castlehaven as his lieutenant general, John Burke in Connacht, Owen Roe O'Neill for Ulster, and Gerat Barry in Munster.

Winter 1642–1643

In late 1642 Parliament began to appoint major generals to command associated counties and regional armies. By doing so they brought into general commands such men as the Earl of Stamford, who was given charge of the south-west where he had been based since the early stages of the Edgehill campaign.[66] At the same time his very young son Thomas Lord Grey of Groby was given command of the midland counties. Lord Grey of Wark was given command of the Eastern Association and Ferdinando, Lord Fairfax was appointed commander of the Northern Association with his son, Sir Thomas Fairfax, as his lieutenant general. The Royalists began to undertake similar work, but in many ways it would not bear fruit until early the following year. Nevertheless in late 1642 Royalists brought into play a new range of generals, such as William Cavendish, Earl of Newcastle.[67] Newcastle was given command of a vast area of the northern and eastern England, stretching from the Scottish border into East Anglia with 53-year-old James King, Lord Eythin, who had fought alongside Alexander Leslie in the Swedish armies, as his lieutenant general and Sir Thomas Glemham as a colonel general; the lowest general officer rank.[68] To his west William Stanley, Earl of Derby was general in command of the area west of the Pennines.[69] Sir Ralph Hopton was given general command on the south-west, and Spencer Compton, Earl of Northampton, was appointed lieutenant general of Warwickshire and Northamptonshire by the end of the year.[70]

For both sides the appointment of these men to regional generalship created a new category of general to add to the field army cadre established in the summer; but it was

King's army, whilst others – presumably those who Whitelocke thought to be politically motivated – urged a chase. Whitelocke, vol. I, pp.192–193.

66 *A True Relation of the proceedings of part of His Majesties forces in Worcester-Shire Shewing how they were encountered by the Right Honourable the Earl of Stamford* (London, 1642), p.1. This journal points out that Stamford had by December 1642 been entrusted to the command of Worcestershire and Hereford.

67 He was already a commissioner of array in four counties: Durham, Staffordshire Nottinghamshire and Northamptonshire. See their various entries in Finch Hatton Mss 133.

68 *ODNB* entries for James King and Sir Thomas Glemham for their biographies. Finch Hatton, 133, Glemham was a commissioner of array for Surrey.

69 Finch Hatton Mss 133, entries for Cheshire, np; Bulstrode Whitelocke, vol. I, p.179. James Stanley, Earl of Derby, was considered so important that both the King and Parliament had chosen him to command the trained bands in Cheshire in winter and spring 1642. Parliament impeached him in August 1642.

70 Northampton was on the commissions of array for both Northamptonshire and Gloucestershire. Finch Hatton Mss 133, entries for Northamptonshire and Gloucestershire.

also a recognition that both the Militia Ordinance and the commissions of array had failed. Some of these men had been commissioners of array, or in case of the Royalists, were displaced lord lieutenants; and some Parliamentarian regional generals were lord lieutenants appointed back in March 1642. It has to be recognised that these appointments, unlike the general office appointments in the spring and summer of 1642, were often political or at least influenced by social and economic issues. These men had at least initially a very different purpose: they were there to galvanise their various personal contacts into action on behalf of the King or Parliament. Their roles, if they were to continue in them, would change and some would morph into field commanders, and such a phenomenon in military appointments would continue right into the 1650s. However, there is no simple picture; these appointments were not always without problems. The appointment of Lord Fairfax, for instance, was problematic. It angered the lord lieutenant and general of the forces in Lincolnshire, Lord Willoughby of Parham, whose county was subsumed into the Northern Association. Moreover, and perhaps more importantly even at this stage, was that the Fairfaxes' rise to general command angered Sir John Hotham, the first man to risk his life defying the King when he had refused him access to Hull and its magazine. Hotham regarded the Fairfaxes as faint hearts – it had taken some time for them to commit themselves fully to Parliament's cause in the north.

There was a mixed bag of experience amongst the new men. Newcastle had none apart from his extensive experience of horse training and management which had all be practised under peacetime conditions. He needed the experience of those who were to serve under him, Lord Eythin and Glemham. James King, Lord Eythin, was a 52-year-old veteran had a great deal of experience: he had served in the Swedish army as long ago as 1609, had been appointed a major general in 1632 and a few years later was lieutenant general to Alexander Leslie in Westphalia and received a Swedish knighthood. He was able to bring the defeated horse under his command off from the fray at the battle of Lemgo when Prince Rupert was captured; Rupert blamed him for his capture. Glemham, aged 42, had also experienced war on the Continent and had served with the Duke of Buckingham's Île de Re expedition in the 1620s; he also had experience as a deputy lieutenant in Suffolk.[71] The Fairfaxes by contrast with Newcastle were quite different having been brought up in a family with considerable military experience. Lord Fairfax was 57 years old, had experience of fighting in the Dutch Wars, and had been a colonel in the Scottish Wars. His 30-year-old son, Sir Thomas Fairfax, had also served on the Continent with Sir Horace Vere, alongside his

71 Clarendon, vol. II, p.286.

rival in 1642, John Hotham junior.[72] Parliament appointed both Ferdinando and Sir Thomas to the Yorkshire county committee in 1642.[73]

In the south midlands, the Earl of Northampton was a of a similar age to Glemham and had also served on the Continent: with a commission in Lord Goring's horse he had been involved in the siege at Breda in 1637, and in 1638 he had fought in the Elector Palatine's army at the Battle of Vlotho in 1638. At home he had served as Lord Lieutenant from 1630 onwards. In the south-west the appointment of Sir Ralph Hopton as lieutenant general in November 1642 was also based on the firm foundation of experience. Like his great rival in the war Sir William Waller, he had served the King's sister in the Palatinate in the early 1620s. By 1626 he was Sir Charles Rich's lieutenant colonel in Count Mansfeld's expedition on the Continent. Thereafter his military service was as a deputy lieutenant for the county of Somerse. Hopton's opposite number, Waller, was of a similar age to Sir Ralph. He saw action as early as 1617, before becoming involved in the early stages of the Thirty Years' War. In the Civil War he had received an early commission in Parliament's horse, with which he had served at Edgehill and was caught up in the defeat. Thereafter he was given command in the west to try to halt the Royalists' success there, ironically led by his old friend and comrade in arms.There were other generals who may have been appointed to general officer commands late in the year: for example Sir John Meldrum, one of the brigade commanders in Essex's army at Edgehill, was a Scot about whom little is know. He was probably born before 1598, making him in his fifties at least by the outbreak of war.[74] He had served in Ireland in 1617, and by the end of the 1630s he was in the service of Sweden, having been on the Continent since the 1620s, and served Gustavus Adolphus as a colonel of a foot regiment at the end of that decade. He would certainly be a major general by early 1643.

The Early War Generals

The first generals of the Civil War were a mixed collection of men, some with years of experience and some with none at all. In terms of non-military background and experience they were likewise a mixed bunch. Over half of the generals had received higher education at some level, either at one of the two English universities and/or Gray's Inn, one of the Inns of Court. Only one 1640 general and the 1642 Parliamentarian generals seem to have taken the latter legal-education route, but the Royalist officers were more likely to have attended a university college. Ten of the fourteen 1640 Royalists who went to university went to Cambridge, with Queens College and Magdalen attracting two each, whilst the Earl of Newcastle and two others attended St John's. Cambridge was

72 Hopper, Andrew, *Black Tom: Sir Thomas Fairfax and the English Revolution* (Manchester: Manchester University Press, 2007), pp.16–17.

73 Finch Hatton, Mss 133, entry for Yorkshire. Ferdinando and Thomas were appointed to the first committee in February 1643, but Ferdinando was on a committee for disarming papists a year earlier, tasked with the role in the West Riding. His son was given a role on the committee for York in February 1642, a post that would have little point to it until July 1644.

74 *ODNB*, entry for Sir John Meldrum.

also the most popular institution for the Parliamentarian generals. Amongst the four who attended university, three of the four – Thomas Fairfax, the Earl of Stamford and John Meyrick – went there whilst Essex attended Oxford. The ages of the generals is apparent from the higher education experience, for example the youngest general, Lord Grey, seems to have attended neither of the universities, but he did go to Gray's Inn like his father.[75] Amongst this cadre, age was clearly important; with the exception of Grey these were mature men with years of accumulated experience. In the vast majority of cases, this is reflected in the levels of experience in government and administration as it is clearly age related. The older generals were, at this stage of their lives and careers, heads of their respective families and because of this had served in a variety of political and administrative offices before the outbreak of Civil War in 1642. On both sides there were men who had been elected MPs, eight Royalists and seven Parliamentarians, and of course the titled generals had also sat in the House of Lords. At this stage in the war most of these men had a claim to be a pillar of their community and because of their age and status within their families, and reinforced by their family's position in society, they were men who held office. In terms of county administration there was a gamut of experience: at least four Parliamentarians and three Royalists had served as a justices of the peace. The Fairfaxes, father and son, are an example. Lord Fairfax had been an MP from the Addled Parliament of 1614 through to the Short and Long Parliaments of 1640 (this was only possible in the later years because his was a Scottish title) and he had been a JP of long standing. His son Sir Thomas had much less experience because his father was still alive and holding the offices which would be the prerogative of the family. The same is also true of the Greys of Groby, the Earl of Stamford and Thomas Lord Grey his heir. The father had been a JP of long standing and a deputy lieutenant. Even though his son was very young, his family's stance as enemies of the Hastings family had helped him secure a parliamentary seat in 1640, promoted by Huntingdon's enemies.[76] The same was true of the Parliamentarian Earl of Bedford. He had only become an MP in the same year as Lord Grey of Groby, 1640, due to his youth (he was 26 in 1642) and because his father, who died in 1641, had until his death held the offices normally accruing to the family. Despite this Bedford had already been appointed to the role of lord lieutenant for Devon in March 1642.[77] This situation was only true of the 1640 class and early Civil War appointees to general rank. As the war progressed this would change. The age profile would shift downwards with about 60 percent of the Civil War generals being in their 20s and 30s. The levels of social experience likewise declined across the board as these men were young enough to have living fathers, like

75 Richards, Jeffrey, *Aristocrat and Regicide, The Life and Times of Thomas Lord Grey of Groby* (London: New Millennium, 2000), pp.14–15.

76 For a discussion of this family rivalry see Fleming, D., 'Faction and Civil War in Leicestershire', *Transactions of the Leicestershire Archaeological and Historical Society,* LVII, 1982.

77 Finch Hatton, Ms 133, pages for Devon, np.

Lord Grey in 1642, and were likely to be still in positions of responsibility in their communities on the eve of war.

The first class of generals also began to embrace several categories. There were the magnate generals: Northumberland, Arundel, Wentworth, Holland, Conway, Essex, Newcastle, Stamford, Willoughby of Parham, Lindsey, and Northampton who were appointed because of their social standing at least as much as their zeal. There were the 'swordsman' generals, Skippon, Astley, Ruthven, Ferdinando and Thomas Fairfax appointed because their zeal for the cause was complemented by their proven ability as a soldier and commander of men. Beginning to emerge was the substitute-magnate generals who were their because their fathers were not: Lord Grey of Groby, with very little apart from his zeal and his very brief parliamentary career, was appointed to the rank of major general simply because his father, the Earl of Stamford – appointed lord lieutenant to oust the Hastings family from the office in 1642 – was serving in the south-west as a general of Parliament's forces there. Lord Grey would not be alone, for the scion of the Hastings family, the Earl of Huntingdon, did not lift a finger to defend his king or his family in 1642 and it would be his second son who would a few months later become a magnate-substitute general in the "class of '43". The selection of the regional commanders followed some of the precepts apparent in the appointments of the field army generals during 1642: men of experience were at a premium even if there was great store put on the regional social and economic standing.

Conclusion

As to whether this was England turned Germany, it is more the case that disparate elements of German experience were brought into England and Wales: there were many German fields of conflict to choose from and all of them had relevance here. The months covered by this chapter were, of course, still despite the two wars of 1639 and 1640 and the war in Ireland, the early stages of a war which was to last twice as long as World War Two. Both sides had a long way to go in the development of command structures. This early collection of general officer appointments was, it can be argued, not a bad stab at creating such structures and it followed lines which we can readily understand. True, some of the careers of these early appointees were short lived. Lindsey died, partly at least, because of a conflict in management level in the King's army – a problem which would not go away during the ensuing years. The career of the Earl of Stamford ended in failure within six months of Edgehill, and his son was ousted as a commander during the first Civil War, but later he would assist Cromwell – the man who did most to end his early career – in the magnificent Worcester campaign of 1651. Equally there were some notable successes: Rupert, Forth and Essex fought long and hard for their causes and with some success. Others showed promise of things to come: Philip Skippon created an excellent reputation for himself. New generals would emerge in the next few months, but their ilk would be different. They had been involved in the traumatic campaign of 1642 and honed their skills then. These new men would be tasked with raising new forces in areas where the King and Parliament had already raised their first armies; they would have to bring together the patchwork of garrisons, outposts and fortified homes which until that point made up the rag-tag war. This was to be the rise of the swordsman general and the regional commanders. It is a story for another time and place.

4

'They have sent to Holland for Engineers'

David Flintham

On 13 March 1643, whilst observing the construction of the fortifications around London, Gerolamo Agostini, the Venetian Ambassador, reported that the authorities had 'sent to Holland for Engineers'[1] to advise on the design and construction on the capital's defences. This was something repeated across the country, and as Lieutenant-Colonel W.G. Ross, R.E. wrote in 1884, 'To Military Engineering … as practised in England during the seventeenth century, the general remark applies that the methods employed were essentially those used and originated by foreigners.'[2]

But foreign involvement in the design and construction of British fortifications was not a phenomenon of the mid 17th century, nor was it a purely an English preserve. Foreign engineers had heavily influenced fortress design during the Tudor era, and these foreign experts had themselves been influenced and gained experience from others. This was part of a Europe-wide evolution in fortress warfare, something which is probably most marked in the transition in fortress design from something practised by the great artists of the Renaissance to a science to be practised by mathematicians and others, ultimately becoming a vital arm of any modern professional army. Thus, for a proper understanding of foreign practices which were to have such a profound influence on fortress design during the Civil Wars, attention must first be given to its origins.

During the Renaissance, discussion about fortress warfare had initially looked back to classical sources, most notably Caesar's *Gallic Wars*, and the account of his successful siege of Alesia in 52BC. The design of fortifications was taken on by artists (Leonardo da Vinci made sketches for the fortifications at Piombino in 1504, and

1 *Calendar of State Papers, Venetian*, 1642–43, reprinted as *The English Civil War – A Contemporary Account* (London: Caliban Books, 1996), Volume 3, 1643–47, p. 29.

2 Lieutenant-Colonel W.G. Ross, RE, in *Military Engineering during the Great Civil War, 1642–1649*, reprinted in the Ken Trotman Military History Monographs series (London: Ken Trotman, 1984), p. 9.

Michelangelo produced a design for the walls of Florence in 1526),[3] something which has led some to look upon fortress engineering as an art form, rather than a science. The architects Brunelleschi and Buontalenti both designed fortifications, and in his *Il Principe* (*The Prince* – 1513) Niccolo Machiavelli considered the role of fortifications as a means of maintaining control of the population,[4] something that would be echoed in London nearly a century and a half later,[5] whilst his *Arte della Guerra* (1520–1) considered the design of fortifications to resist artillery.[6] Outside Italy, just before his death, the German artist and theorist Albrecht Dürer wrote his *Etliche Unterricht, zur Befestigung der Städte, Schlosser und Flecken* (*Instruction on the Fortification of Cities, Castles, and Towns* – 1527), which was probably the final word (with one or two exceptions) on the 'drum'-style artillery tower until the advent of the Martello Tower at the end of the 18th century.

Thus, military engineering during the 16th century was significantly dominated by Italians who shared their knowledge through a number of treatises on military engineering, including Galasso Alghisi's *Delle Fortificationi* (1570), Antonio Lupicini's *Architettura Militare* (1582), Girolamo Maggi and Giacomo *Castriotto's Della Fortificatione delle citta* (1583), and Buonaiuto Lorino's *Le Fortificationi* (1596 – Lorino had designed fortifications for France, Spain and Venice).[7] Francesco Tensini had carried out works at Bergamo, Crema, Peshiera, and Verona, and in 1624 wrote *La Fortificatione Gvardia Difesa et Espvgnatione delle Fortezze esperimentata in diverse guerre.*[8] Diego Ufano's *Tratado de Artilleria*, which was published in Brussels in 1613 was highly influential, and was plundered shamelessly by English writers such as Henry Hexham and Robert Ward.[9] In his *Anima'dversions of War* of 1639, Ward wrote:

> the bulwarkes are the Head, the Flanckers the Eyes, the Curtins the Armes, and so the other parts. Now if the Head bee not wel-disposed then all the other members will be found ill: even so those bulwarkes which are not formed according to the disposition which is requisite all the fortress is imperfect.[10]

3 J.R. Hale, *Renaissance Fortification: Art or Engineering?* (London: Thames and Hudson, 1977), p.15.
4 Hale, p. 70.
5 *The English Civil War – A Contemporary Account*, Volume 3, p. 33.
6 Hale, p. 71.
7 Hale, p. 70.
8 Hale, p. 31.
9 Christopher Duffy, *Siege Warfare: The Fortress in the Early Modern World, 1494–1660* (London: Routledge and Kegan Paul, 1979), p. 64, and p. 146.
10 Robert Ward, in David R. Lawrence, *The Complete Soldier – Military Books and Military Culture in Early Stuart England*, 1603–1645 (Leiden: Koninklijke Brill NV, 2009), pp. 341–2.

Here, Ward was echoing the theorists of the Italian Renaissance a century before who had highlighted the anatomy of the fortress, most notably Francesco di Giorgio's 'fortress man' and its resemblance to the fortress of Poggio Imperiale.[11]

The demands for more sophisticated fortifications resulted in the applications of a more scientific approach, particularly the use of mathematics (the importance of mathematics to military engineering was due in a large part to the need to calculate covering angles in the design of bastions and the subsequent location of cannon). During the second half of the 16th century, a number of (chiefly Italian) mathematicians wrote treatises on fortifications, including Pietro Cataneo's *I Quattro Primi Libri di Archittectura* (1569), and Carlo Teti's *Discorsi di Fortificationi* (1569). The Frenchman Samuel Marolois' *Fortification ou Architecture Militaire tant Offensive que deffensive* of 1628 was actually originally published as part of his *Oeuvres Mathematiques* (1614).

Maurice, Prince of Orange (1567–1625) also appreciated the importance of mathematics to fortress design, and in 1604, he approached Simon Stevin (1548–1620), a Dutch mathematician, to design a 'blueprint' for future fortifications and siegeworks. Stevin produced standard designs for fortifications and camps (the latter were heavily influenced by the marching camps of the armies of ancient Rome).[12] He later founded a chair for land-surveying at Leiden University (Leiden University was the centre of Dutch learning, an honour bestowed by William the Silent, Prince of Orange, as a reward for its bravery in resisting a siege by the Hapsburgs in 1572).[13] Amongst those who studied at Leiden was the Polish-born mathematician Nikolaus Goldman (1611–55) who published *La nouvelle fortification* in 1645.[14] So, when the Norfolk physician and mathematician Richard Clampe became a military engineer in the Army of the Eastern Association in 1643, he was continuing a tradition that dated back at least 80 years. The relationship between military engineering and mathematics would continue throughout the 17th century.

By the second half of the 16th century military engineering had become a science, dominated no longer by gifted amateurs, but by professional engineers who were a vital component of any army. As military engineering became more scientific, the developing 'breed' of professional military engineers began to look disparagingly at their 'gifted amateur' colleagues. The Englishman, Thomas Malthus had learnt about the explosive mortar bomb during his service with the Dutch during the 1620s. Transferring to French service, he put his learning into a book (he would later bring out an edition in English) 'to confound and ruinate rebels and their habitations; so that afterwards empires, kingdoms, and commonwealths may the better live in peace and

11 Hale, pp. 42–3.

12 Bouko de Groot, *Dutch Armies of the 80 Year's War, 1568–1648*, Volume 2 (Oxford: Osprey Publishing, 2017), pp. 22–23.

13 Margaret Willes, *The Curious World of Samuel Pepys and John Evelyn* (New Haven: Yale University Press, 2018), p.14.

14 Jeremy Black, *Fortifications and Siegecraft: Defence and Attack through the Ages* (London: Rowman and Littlefield, 2018), p. 99.

tranquillity.'[15] The mortar bomb which Malthus introduced into France from the Netherlands was first used at the siege of La Mothe in Lorraine in 1634. Malthus' influence on French bombardier officers last a generation after his death in 1658 (he died during the second siege of Gravelines). But François Blondel ('the Great Blondel'), the French mathematician and military and civil engineer and architect, expressed his dismay in 1685 when he wrote:

> All his [Malthus] knowledge was derived entirely from experience, and he had not the slightest acquaintance with mathematics... He adjusted his mortars by a process of luck and rough calculation, making a guess as to the range, and elevating the barrel accordingly.[16]

4.1 Maurice, Prince of Orange, from the workshop of Michiel Jansz van Mierevelt. (Rijksmuseum, Amsterdam)

Nevertheless, Malthus is notable as he is probably the one English authority who enjoyed any prestige on the Continent.

In Britain, Continental techniques and expertise had influenced every period of artillery fortification construction from the early examples at Canterbury and Norwich onwards, demonstrating a continual flow of ideas and influences from overseas. Whilst these were often, especially at first, executed by foreign experts, they were ultimately implemented by the small number of 'homegrown' military engineers. During the 16th century, fortifications came in two distinct periods: 'the fortifications on the south coast built under Henry VIII were essentially gun platforms. The bastioned enceinte was added during Elizabeth's reign as part of the anti-invasion measures.'[17]

Henry VIII's defence programme of the 1530s and 40s (more correctly known as *Device by the King*), would eventually comprise of some 30 separate fortifications: the

15 Duffy, p. 146.
16 Duffy, p. 138.
17 Black, p. 93.

4.2 Deal Castle. One of the Device by the King forts of the 1530s and 40s. Designed, or at least influenced by the Bohemian architect, Stevan van Haschenperg. It was besieged in 1648. This view by Wenceslaus Hollar dates from 1639. (University of Toronto)

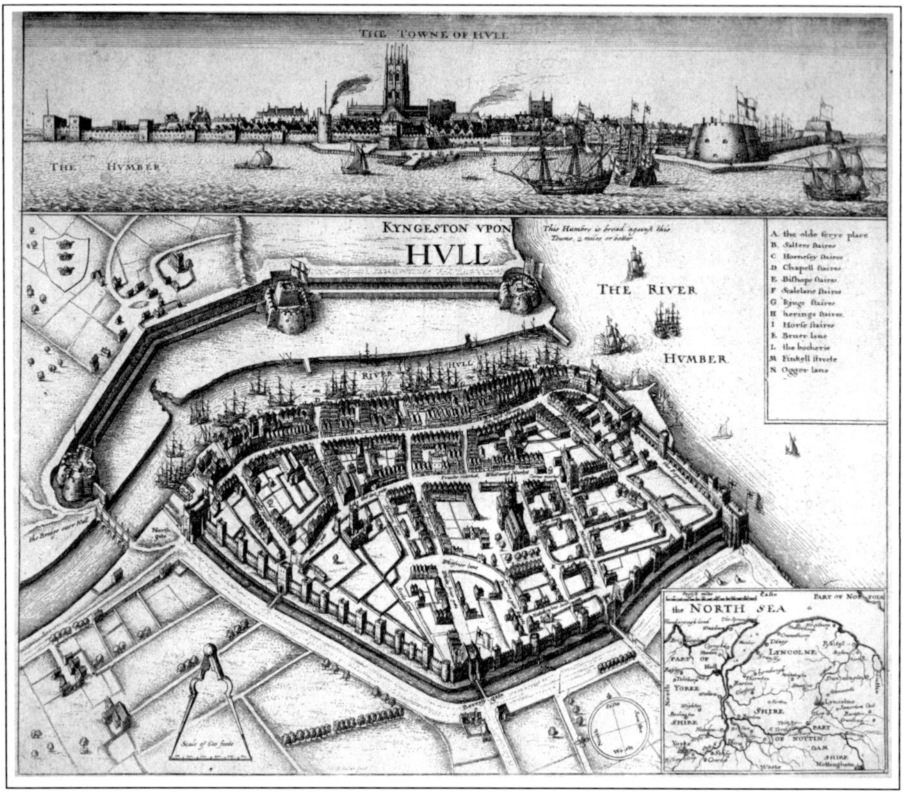

4.3 Wenceslaus Hollar's 1640 plan of Kingston upon Hull, showing John Rogers' design which combined features from both the Italian-type bastioned fortifications and the concentric forts of Henry VIII's *Device* scheme. (University of Toronto)

entrance to Falmouth harbour in Cornwall, Weymouth Bay in Dorset, the Solent in Hampshire, Rye harbour in Sussex, Folkestone, and the Downs anchorage in Kent, the Thames Estuary, Harwich Haven in East Anglia and finally Hull. In Wales, the entrance to Milford Haven was also protected. Whilst the *Device* fortifications were sophisticated by English standards of the time, generally speaking contemporary European artillery fortifications had moved on from the circular to the angular. However, the concept of semi-circular 'roundels' or towers had not completely disappeared from European fortress theory, and had been promoted by Dürer, and whilst his influence was limited across Europe, he did influence the Bohemian architect, Stevan van Haschenperg who was amongst the first of many foreign military architects to find service in England. Van Haschenperg is known to have worked on Sandgate Castle (Folkestone), the modifications to Camber Castle and the citadel of Carlisle. He probably also influenced the designs of the castles at Deal, Walmer and St Mawes as well. In addition to Van Haschenperg, Henry VIII also employed Girolamo de Treviso, Antonio de Bergamo, and Gian Tomasa Scala.

The Thames defences were simpler, taking the form of artillery blockhouses rather than castles. Designed by James Nedeham (who was described as the 'master and devisers of the works' of the Thames bulwarks),[18] and Christopher Morice. A notable fortification on the Kent side of the Thames was at Milton as in 1545, it was modified by Sir Richard Lee with the addition of an angular bastion. Further north, the fortifications designed by John Rogers at Hull in 1541 combined features from both the Italian-type bastioned fortifications and the concentric forts of Henry VIII's *Device* scheme, thus representing a noteworthy milestone in the development of English fortifications.

Having seen Continental fortress design for himself when war broke out with France in 1544 and he led an army to besiege Boulogne, Henry VIII's interest in military engineering was sufficient enough for him to create a seat of military architecture in his Office of Works where the likes of Rogers, Lee and Sir Henry Cavendish followed in Van Haschenperg's footsteps. Importantly, it was through the Office of Works that English fortress design evolved from the circular 'reinforced castle' style of the *Device* castles to the bastion system which was dominating European fortress design.

Although Henry VIII employed Italian engineers, it was his two English engineers, Rogers and Lee, on whom Henry ultimately relied. As Andrew Saunders succinctly summarised, in terms of military engineering, 'the ideas were drawn from foreigners but their execution was entrusted to Englishmen':[19] both Lee and Rogers 'were quite abreast of the continental developments in the science of fortifications'.[20]

The construction of costal defences did not end with Henry's death. During the 1550s, construction began on a state-of-the-art bastioned fort on St Marys (the main island of the Isles of Scilly) – known as *Harry's Walls*, it was never completed. Even further afield, new defensive schemes were also designed and implemented by Rogers in the Channel Islands. North of the border, the port of Leith was protected by a system of fortifications of French design and construction which were, at the time, the most modern fortifications to be found anywhere in the British Isles.[21]

During the first years of the reign of Elizabeth I, new fortifications constructed at just two locations: Upnor Castle on the River Medway in Kent, and Berwick-upon-Tweed. Upnor, opposite Chatham dockyard, represents something of a 'transitional' design. Lee's castle had a number of features which hark back to an earlier age including partial bastions and tall, slender angle turrets. Berwick, on the other hand, was a landward (rather than a purely coastal) fortification, and would be in the front line should an

18 Peter Harrington, *The Castles of Henry VIII* (Oxford: Osprey Publishing, 2007), p. 15.

19 Andrew Saunders, *Fortress Britain: Artillery Fortification in the British Isles and Ireland* (Liphook: Beaufort Publishing, 1989), p. 52.

20 L.R. Shelby, *John Rogers: Tudor Military Engineer* (Oxford: Oxford University Press, 1967), p. 144.

21 David Flintham, 'The Fortifications of Leith, 1558–1916', in *Fort 41* (Fortress Study Group, 2013), pp. 93–4.

incursion from Scotland occur. In 1550, Lee and Sir Thomas Palmer were charged with improving Berwick's defences, but Lee's plans were flawed, yet redesigning the defences was expensive and would take time. Work limped along until 1569, (and required foreign expertise as well: Giovanni Portarini and Jacopo Contio both worked on the fortifications). Thus, Berwick's defences ended up as something of a compromise, but despite this, they are impressive to this day and represent the nearest England came to a Continental-style fortified town.[22] Indeed, the only towns to be fortified in a systematic and scientific manner during the Tudor period were Berwick and Portsmouth, the latter having its defences completely revised in 1580, and were reconstructed as a bastioned trace, incorporating both landward and harbour defences.

The Armada crisis of the 1580s and 90s prompted a major increase in fortress construction (and expenditure), and the involvement of engineers, both foreign and English. Federigo Giambelli, best known for his 'infernal machines' which destroyed the Spanish boom at Antwerp in 1585, attempted, unsuccessfully, to construct a boom between Tilbury and Gravesend. Fortifications were hurriedly constructed elsewhere: on the Isle of Wight, for instance, the medieval defences of Carisbrooke Castle were strengthened, although it was not until 1597 that the castle's defences were completely revised, Giambelli enclosing the castle in a circuit of ramparts and ditch, a mile in length, and including five bastions (the eastern and south-west bastions included two-story flanker batteries).

The later Elizabethan period is dominated by two engineers, Robert Adams and Paul Ive. Adams was involved in the redesign of Portsmouth's defences and designed *Star Castle*, an eight-pointed star-shaped fort on the Hugh, the headland to the west of St Mary's harbour on the Scilly Isles. But his most significant works were at Plymouth where he designed the first fort on the Hoe in 1592. Ive was employed in the Channel Islands in 1593–5 and then carried out improvements to Pendennis Castle. But he is best known for his treatise *The Practice of Fortifications* (1589), the first by a native engineer. Whilst his designs still showed some Italian influence, he drew heavily on his experience in the Low Countries, and his work represents a landmark in British military engineering: no longer were English military men ignorant of European warfare or completely reliant on foreign experts.

The accession of James VI/I in 1603, heralded a period of stagnation in British military engineering. Whilst the first 40 years of the 17th century did witness some fortress construction, for instance in 1602, after the siege of Kinsale, the Paul Ive-designed *James Fort* (named in honour of the King) was built to protect the harbour (it was completed by 1607), it is safe to say that during the period, Britain did slip behind Continental practice.

Thus, at the outbreak of the English Civil War, few comparatively modern fortifications existed in England. Save for some isolated coastal or estuary blockhouses and forts, it was only Berwick-upon-Tweed, Plymouth and Portsmouth (the latter,

22 Saunders, *Fortress Britain*, pp. 57–61.

according to Clarendon, was 'the strongest and best fortified town then in the Kingdom')[23] could be considered 'modern'. Inland, there were a number of towns which still processed their Roman or Medieval town walls (despite the comment of Frederich, Duke of Württemberg in 1592 who noted that all English towns were 'without walls'), although as Robert Ward noted in his 1639 *Anima'dversions of War*, 'we may not be deceived in putting our confidence in the strength of them'.[24]

The last time there had been any sieges in the British Isles had been in Ireland during the Nine Years' War (the final siege of the conflict was the siege of Dunboy Castle, 5–18 June 1602. This was five months after the more famous siege and battle of Kinsale, 2 October 1601–3 January 1602). But the Nine Years' War did not provide a significant insight into contemporary Continental fortress warfare methods. So, as the threat of Civil War in Britain intensified, attention turned to the practices employed during the Eighty Years' War and the Thirty Years' War. Thus, it was the methods of Maurice and Frederick Henry, Prince of Orange in the Netherlands, and the Swedish King, Gustavus Adolphus which were to have the far-reaching influences – generally speaking the Dutch was the predominate influence for the English, whilst the Scots tended to be more influenced by the Swedes.[25] Whilst a generalisation, the Dutch demonstrated a far greater preference for sieges and fortresses than the Swedes, who preferred to give battle, although this is not to say that the Dutch did not fight battles (although their defeat at Kallo in 1638, in which was the largest pitched battle of the entire Eighty Years' War, demonstrated the need to avoid battles in the future) or the Swedes conduct sieges.

John Cruso (1592–after 1655) in his *Art of Warre* of 1639 groups the whole of foreign practice into four principle divisions or schools, viz.: French, Spanish, Italian, and Dutch.[26] Many of his works were as editor and a translator of Continental works, the Oxford Dictionary of National Biography notes that 'Cruso's military works were significant only in that they were the first to make the new continental, primarily Dutch, military literature available to an English-speaking audience.'[27]

Robert Ward in his *Anima'dversions of War* (1639) considered that the Dutch or 'Low-country manner' the 'most absolutest manner that can be invented.'[28] Having examined the plans of works constructed during the war Ross concludes that it was the Dutch method which was most closely followed by English engineers during the Civil Wars (despite the fact that Continental sieges could go on for years as exemplified by the sieges of Rijnberk in 1586–90 and Ostend, 1601–04). The enceinte constructed round Oxford is perhaps the most important example of the Dutch school during the entire Civil

23 Quoted by Ross, p. 17.
24 Ross, p. 18.
25 Duffy, p. 145.
26 Ross, p. 12.
27 Grell, Ole Peter (2004), 'Cruso, John (fl. 1595–1655)', *Oxford Dictionary of National Biography* (online edn.). Oxford University Press. doi:10.1093/ref:odnb/6852
28 Ross, p. 14.

4.4 (right, top): a plan of the 1624 siege of Breda.
4.5 (right, bottom): a plan of the 1637 siege of Breda from the workshop of Claes Jansz. Visscher. (Both from Rijksmuseum, Amsterdam)

War period. But this distinctive Dutch school of military engineering, which was such a great influence on military engineering during the Civil Wars, was itself still developing during the early years of the 17th century and owed much to the likes of Stevin, Adam Freitag (author of the 1631 *Architectura militaries nova et aucta*) and Christian Otter.

Given the topography of the Netherlands, it is of no surprise that it was the earthen rampart and ditch, commonly wet, that were the dominant characteristics of Dutch fortifications. Another advantage was the relatively low cost of earthwork fortifications. From this, Maurice developed the complete earthen enceinte. Ideally, the thick earth rampart, with its unrevetted scarp, would be some 7.6 metres high, protected from scaling by storm poles (sharpened horizontal palisades). About 4.5 metres from the rampart was the *fausee-braye*, a low, outer rampart which protected the foot of the main rampart, and commanded the ditch, and 'covered-way' beyond. The ditch or wet-moat would be 46 metres wide and occasionally include a *cunette*, an additional vertical sided ditch, six metres wide, running down the centre of the main ditch. Next, on the counterscarp of the ditch, was the covered-way, a continuous protected path, with a parapet which overlooked the sloping glacis beyond.[29] This represented the ideal which was rarely, if ever, achieved in Britain during the Civil Wars. Indeed, there is only a single known plan which sets out this full Dutch method: Clampe's design for the southern defences at King's Lynn, *c.*1643–4.[30]

Since Clampe's plan features just a single bastion, it is not possible to gauge how this fits into the Dutch model where the bastion's salient angle would vary between 60° in a square figure to 90° in a dodecagon. The faces of the bastion would meet in narrow salient angles that could be sued to supplement the cross-fire of the bastion flanks. The line from the point of junction between one bastion and the next, known as the 'line of defence' was devised according to the range of musketry, so would be no longer than 220 metres. But whilst this was accepted in theory, this was a level of sophistication seldom achieved in Britain, with only the plans for King's Lynn, Newport Pagnell and Oxford recognised as being the most compliant to this Dutch model. Even scarcer was the use of complex outer-works, such as 'half-moon' (*demi-lunes*) bastions which were set in front of the principle bastions, 'hornworks' (with demi-bastions), and 'crownworks' (with full bastions). Far more common in a British context was the

29 Saunders, *Fortress Britain*, pp. 72–3, and Michael Osborne, *Sieges and Fortifications of the Civil Wars in Britain*, (Leigh-on-Sea: Partizan Press, 2004), p. 8.

30 David Flintham, 'Richard Clampe, *c.*1617–1696', in *Fort* (Fortress Study Group, 2019), to be published. How (or for that matter, if) Clampe's plans were implemented is one of the objectives of the Kings Lynn under Siege English Civil War Archaeological Project (see <https://www.militaryhistorylive.co.uk/mhl-kings-lynn-under-siege.html>).

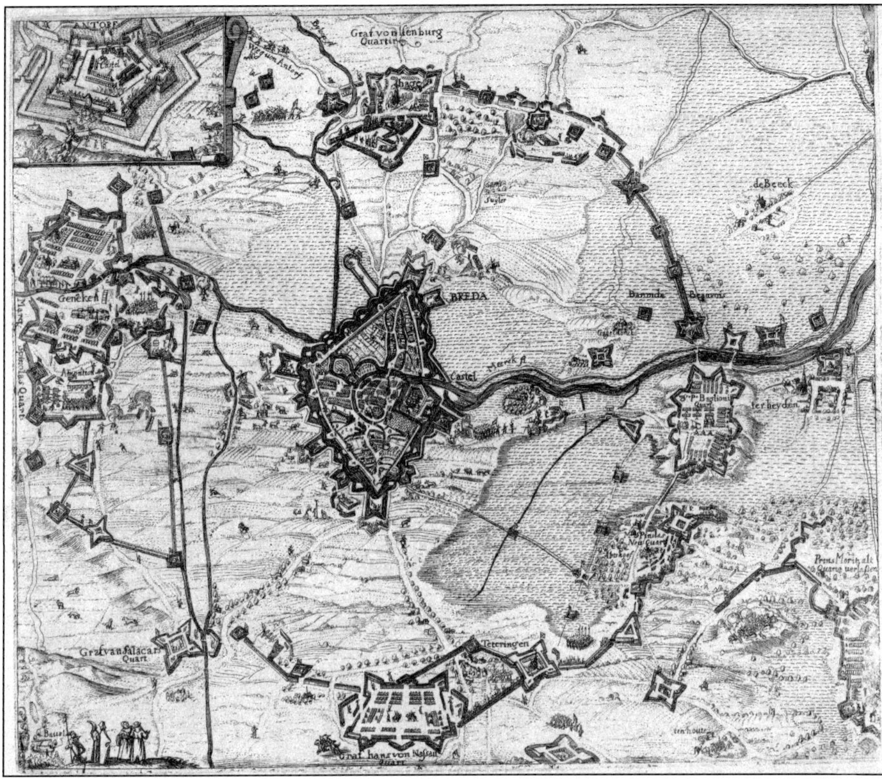
BREDA
Geneken
deBeeck
ter heyden
Teteringen
Castel

Nieuwe Kaerte van BREDA
B R A B A N
H O L
L A N
D I Æ
P A R S.
Houtse Duynen
Oosterhout

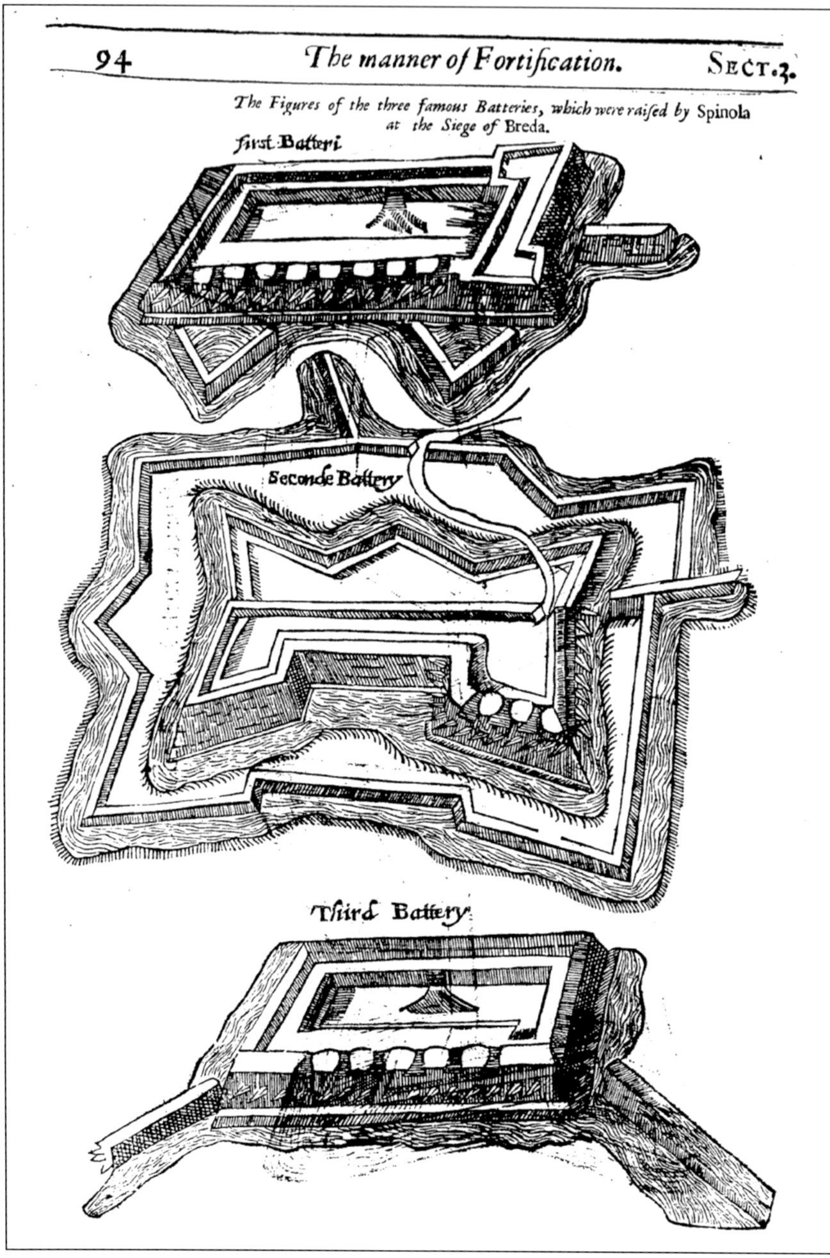

4.6 Illustrations of batteries at Breda, from Richard Ward's *Anima'dversions of Warre* (1639).

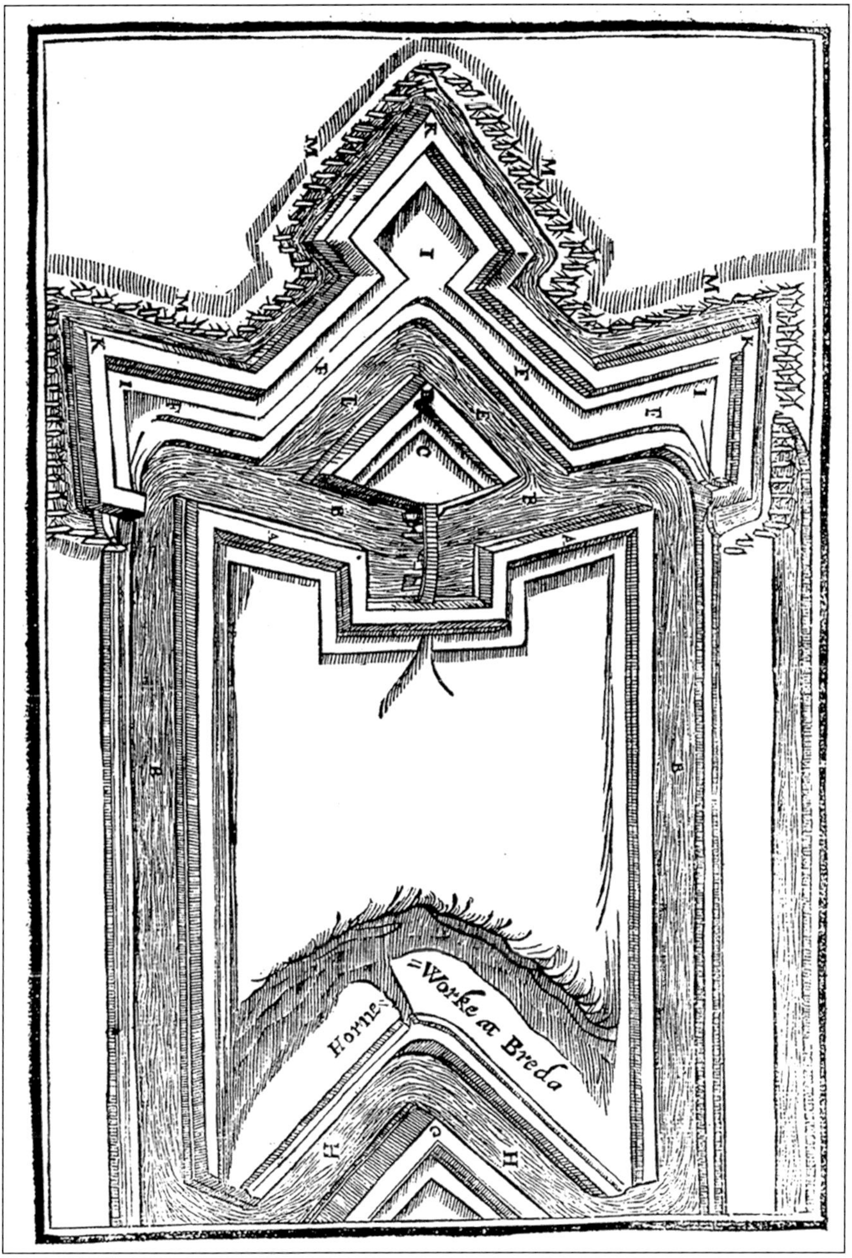

4.7 Illustration of a hornwork at Breda, from Richard Ward's *Anima'dversions of Warre* (1639).

schans (or 'sconce', to give it its common English name), a (relatively) small earthen redoubt, normally independently situated, constructed to control key strategic features such as river crossings.

Amongst the other innovations introduced by Maurice was the bridging train and pontoon which enabled narrow waterways to be crossed easily (unsurprising given the terrain of the Low Countries) and providing the necessary tools and equipment to convert small vessels into a bridge-of-boats should larger waterways be encountered. Thus, although lands could be flooded as a form of defence, such measures need not halt the designs of a besieging army as the Dutch demonstrated at Den Bosch in 1629 (when they drained a swamp) and Breda in 1637 (when they diverted a river). Under Maurice, fascines were standardised (these measured 3 x 1.8 m; the size of gabions and even sandbags were also regulated), and various weapons for trench warfare which would not have been out of place during World War One appeared. Whilst not a Dutch invention, the hand grenade was another weapon that was developed during the Eighty Years' War: noted at Steenwijiki in 1592, by the 1630s, a properly stocked fortification for 3,000 men was supposed to have 1,200 2.5 kg hand grenades. John Maurice of Nassau (1604–1679) even proposed the creation of small grenadier units.[31]

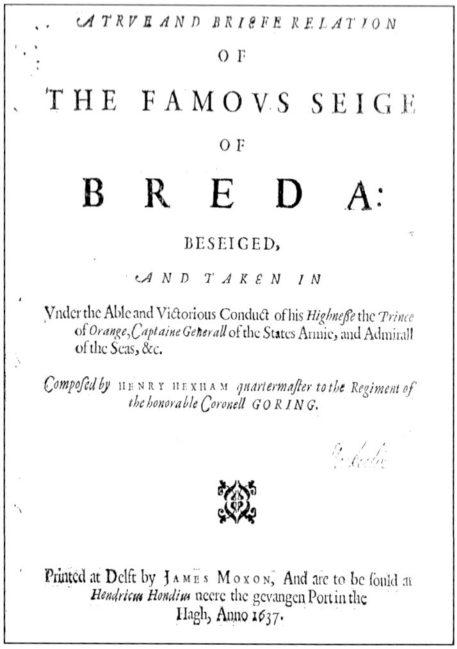
A TRVE AND BRIEFE RELATION
OF
THE FAMOVS SEIGE
OF
BREDA:
BESEIGED,
AND TAKEN IN
Vnder the Able and Victorious Conduct of his Highnesse the Prince of Orange, Captaine Generall of the States Armie, and Admirall of the Seas, &c.
Composed by HENRY HEXHAM quartermaster to the Regiment of the honorable Coronell GORING.
Printed at Delft by JAMES MOXON, And are to be sould at Hendricus Hondius neere the gevangen Port in the Hagh, Anno 1637.

4.8 The cover of Henry Hexham's *The Famous Siege of Breda*, detailing the 1637 siege.

For the English-speaking audience, these advances were described by those who actually participated in the sieges as part of the numerous volunteer forces (such as Robert Barret who wrote *The Theorike and Practike of Modern Warres* and Francis Markham, author of the 1622 *Five Decades of Epistles of Warre*),[32] employed by all sides, or repeated or translated from others. One of the most noteworthy authors was Henry Hexham who participated at several sieges during the 1620s and 1630s:

> [His] three instructional manuals, *The principles of the art militarie practised in the warres of the United Netherlands* (1637), *The second part of the principles of art military, practised in the warres*

31 de Groot, p. 24 and p. 33.
32 Saunders, *Fortress Britain*, p. 72.

of the United Provinces (1639), and *The third part of the principles of the art militarie practised in the warres of the United Provinces* (1640) were a tour de force of English military literature and a veritable catalogue of the Dutch contribution to the transformation of warfare.[33]

During the 1630s, Hexham also translated Marolois' *Fortification on Architecture militair tant offensive que defensive.*

It is the second of Hexham's three treatises which is the most important from a fortress warfare perspective as it is this one which covered siegecraft in the most detail. It was dedicated to George Goring and it was as quartermaster in Goring's regiment in 1637 that took Hexham to Breda. Hexham had also participated at the sieges of 's-Hertogenbosch (1629), Venlo, and Maastricht (1631–2), witnessing the complexities of Continental siegecraft, and its interplay of engineers, gunners, miners and soldiers[34]. His second treatise also included a diagram of Breda, as well as a description of the preparation of siege-works, including entrenching, whilst his third treatise also examined the technical arts of gunnery and siegecraft.

Arguably no one foreign siege had a greater impact upon fortress warfare in the British Civil Wars than the sieges of the Dutch fortified city of Breda (1624–5 and 1637). The siege of 1624–5 saw Breda fall to the Spanish Army of Flanders under Ambrogio Spinola: the Irishman Gerat (Gerald) Barry served in the *Tercio Irlanda* in the Spanish Army and during the siege he spent most of his time on entrenchments. Following the siege, he produced an unofficial translation of Herman Hugo's Latin *Obsidio Bredana*[35] (Hugo (9 May 1588–11 September 1629) was a Jesuit priest, writer and military chaplain. His *Obsidio Bredana* (1626) was an account of the siege). Barry considered Breda to be the 'seminary ... of the military discipline'.[36] Barry went to serve at Ostend (1631) and Cambrai (1634).

Barry added to the large number of military treatises written during the 1630s which set out to 'quantify the known military world'[37] with his *A discourse of military discipline* (1634). Like a number of his contemporaries, Barry recognised the importance of mathematics to the infantry officer. The third volume of Barry's work covers siegecraft, recognising that specialist explosive, incendiary, and other siege techniques were best left to specialist military engineers. This third volume also included a chapter on fortresses. Barry went on to command the Army of Munster during the Irish Rebellion, during which time he successfully besieged King John's

33 David R. Lawrence, *The Complete Soldier – Military Books and Military Culture in Early Stuart England, 1603–1645* (Leiden: Koninklijke Brill NV, 2009), p. 104.

34 Lawrence, p. 208,

35 Gerat Barry, *The Siege of Breda By the Armies of Phillip the Fovrt under the Government of Isabell Achieved By the Conduct of Ambr Spinola* (Louvain: Ex officina Hastenii, 1627).

36 Lawrence, p. 335.

37 Keith Dowen, 'Gerat Barry' (lecture), *Century of the Soldier Conference*, Royal Armouries, Leeds, 22 September 2018.

4.9 (right, top): A plan of the 1627 siege of Grol. Of particular note is the profile (bottom left) of the Dutch system of fortifications. (Rijksmuseum, Amsterdam)
4.10 (right, bottom): J. Blaeu's map of the Siege of Grol in 1627 features (at the bottom right) the 'Fort des Anglois, Engelsche Schans', a feature subsequently detailed by Hugo de Groot in 1629.

Castle in Limerick, using mining to bring down a section of the castle's walls.[38] Mining was the one form of regular siege warfare where the British excelled their Continental contemporaries.[39]

The official English translation of *Obsidio Bredana* was by Henry Gage (1597–1645), who was a captain in the Spanish Army of Flanders, and had distinguished himself at the siege, but returned to England during the Anglo-Spanish War (1625–30) rather than fight against his own countrymen. In England, he translated Hugo's account, which was published by Judocus Doams in Ghent as *The Siege of Breda*. Hugo's work included plans of Breda's fortifications as well as drawings of the besieging Spanish army's sconces and redoubts, providing an accurate picture of the siegeworks employed during the siege which lasted from August 1624 until June 1625. The siege became a proving ground for the hundreds of British soldiers who fought there, and its eventual capitulation and honourable surrender did nothing to tarnish the reputation of its British defenders, some of whom would return 12 years later.

Before moving on to the 1637 siege, mention should be made of another siege, that of the eastern Dutch city of Grol (also known as Groenlo, Grolle and Grolla) undertaken by Frederick Henry. J. Blaeu's map of the *Siege of Grol* in 1627 features (at the bottom right) the 'Fort des Anglois, Engelsche Schans' (English Sconce), a feature subsequently detailed by Hugo de Groot in 1629. This sconce was constructed and garrisoned by English soldiers in Dutch service, whilst the 'Fransche Schans' (French Sconce) which is also featured on Blaeu's plan, was built and garrisoned by French soldiers.[40]

The Fifth Siege of Breda (21 July–11 October 1637) saw the Stadtholder, Frederick Henry, Prince of Orange, retake the city (although whilst the Dutch were occupied at Breda, the Spanish took the opportunity to capture both Venlo and Roermond). Thereafter, the city would remain in the hands of the Dutch Republic until the end of the war. During the siege, Dutch pioneers were expected to each construct four metres of the line of ramparts, and for the assault itself, they had evolved quite sophisticated assault units to go 'into the breach': the first wave was the storming party designed to take and hold the breach. The storming party comprised of a lieutenant,

38 Kenneth Wiggins, *Siege Mines and Underground Warfare*, (Princes Risborough: Shire Publications Limited, 2003), pp. 35–37, and also Kenneth Wiggins, *Anatomy of a Siege: King John's Castle, Limerick, 1642* (Wicklow: Wordwell Limited, 2000).

39 Duffy, p. 147.

40 The English Sconce is well preserved, whilst the layout of the French Sconce has been traced by the use of aerial photography. See <http://www.engelseschans.nl/> (accessed 08/07/2018).

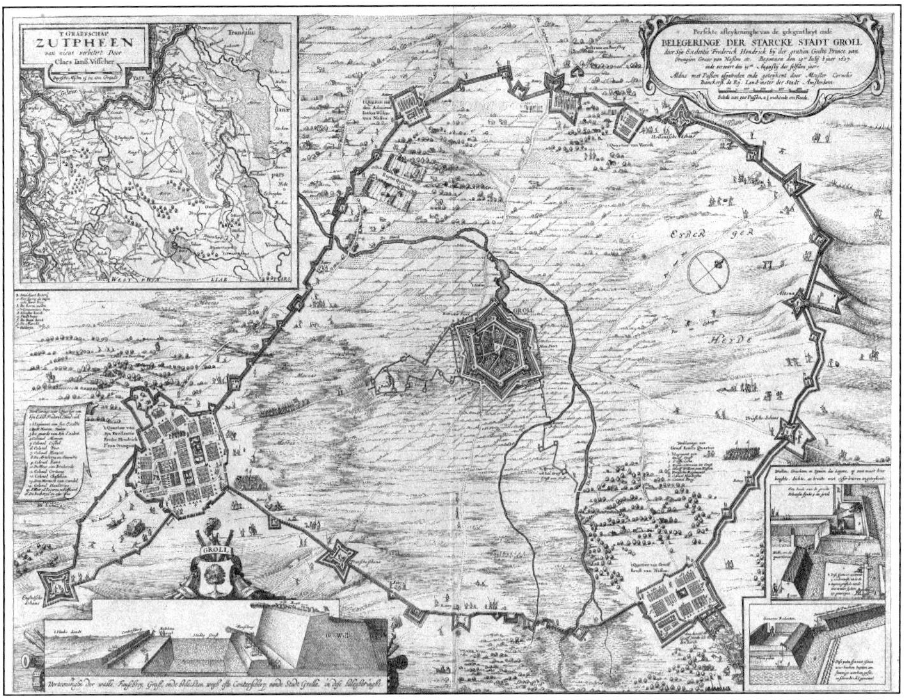
T GRAEFSCHAP ZUTPHEEN
BELEGERINGE DER STARCKE STADT GROLL
GROLL

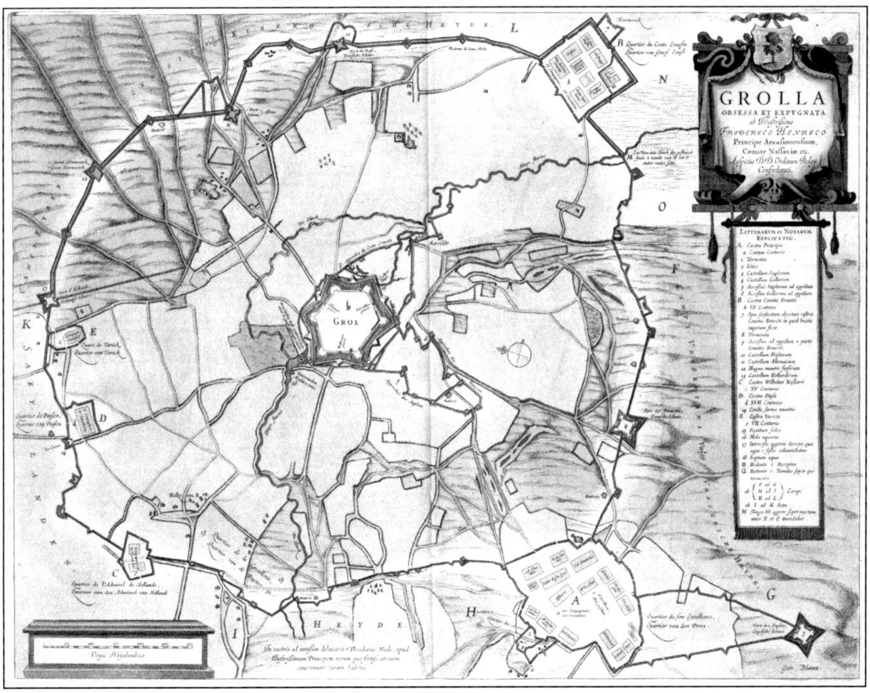
GROLLA
OBSESSA ET EXPVGNATA
GROL

a sergeant, four grenadiers and 50 skirmishers armed with flintlocks and something called a vaulting-spear (its intended purpose is self-explanatory, although how it was actually used is a matter of debate). The storming party was followed by a supporting force comprising of lieutenant, a sergeant and 50 men (at a 1:1 musket to pike ratio). This was followed a second wave, or breakthrough group which was made up of a full company of musketeers and pikemen, supported by 80 pikemen under two sergeants. The remainder of the assault force followed in the third wave and these were followed by a workforce of 100 men to consolidate the captured ground.[41]

This tactic was employed at Breda, and on one occasion the assault was led by Captain George Monck:

> The Prince [of Orange] immediately gave order for the springing of both the mines, and the falling on upon the breaches which the mines should make. The first officer then of the English which was to fall up the breach and to enter it was Captain Monck, Colonel Goring's Captain, with 20 musketeers and 10 pikes, and after him a workmaster13 with certain workmen, to cast up a breast[work] behind them, that they might lodge our men upon the top of the horn-work. Next unto Captain Abrahall and Lieutenant Broome was to fall upon the right hand with forty pikes and 20 musketeers. And Captain Hammond with his Ensign on the left hand, to second Captain Monck, with Captain Abrahall, there fell on these noble volunteers, worthy officers, and cavilleros of the Colonel's Company: my Lord Grandisson, Captain Croft, Captain La Meere, Lieutenant Turuill, Cornet Lucas, Ensign Pagett, Mr. Oneall, Mr. Apsley, Mr. Eldrington, Mr. Symon Fanchy, Mr. Griffin, Mr. Postlumus Kirton, Mr. Evers, Mr. Morley, Mr. Daniell, Mr. Predeaux, Mr. Lenthol, Mr. Wilford, Mr. Bakersfield, Mr. Lyle, and Mr. Watson, with diverse other Gentlemen of quality. This company of pikes kept always together.
>
> The English mine then being sprung, and taking good effect, Captain Monck, ere the smoke was vanished, hastens up to the breach, and with his commanded men, fell up to the very top of it, where at first he was entertained with some musketry of the enemy. But they instantly gave back, and he with his commanded men, of which half had slunk away, advanced forward into the work, where he found a stand of pikes, of about six or seven score, ready to receive him. And falling in pell mell upon them, whether by order, or out of affection for the Colonel [recently wounded in action], or for a revenge upon the enemy, they gave the word 'a Goring, a Goring,' and though the enemy were twice their number, yet Captain Abrahall, being bravely followed with a Company of gallant men, charged home upon them, and came to push of the pike with them. And seeing this advantage, that Captain Monck fell upon the left flank of them, and galled them shordly[?] with his musketeers, Captain Abrahall pressing hard upon them, and this brought the enemy into a disorder, and made them give back. Upon this the French also falling on upon their right flank from their side, diverse of them were slain, drowned and wholly routed.[42]

41 de Groot, p. 34.

42 From: *A True and Brief Relation of the Famous Siege of Breda: besieged, and taken under the able and victorious conduct of his Highness the Prince of Orange, Captain General of the States' Army, and Admiral*

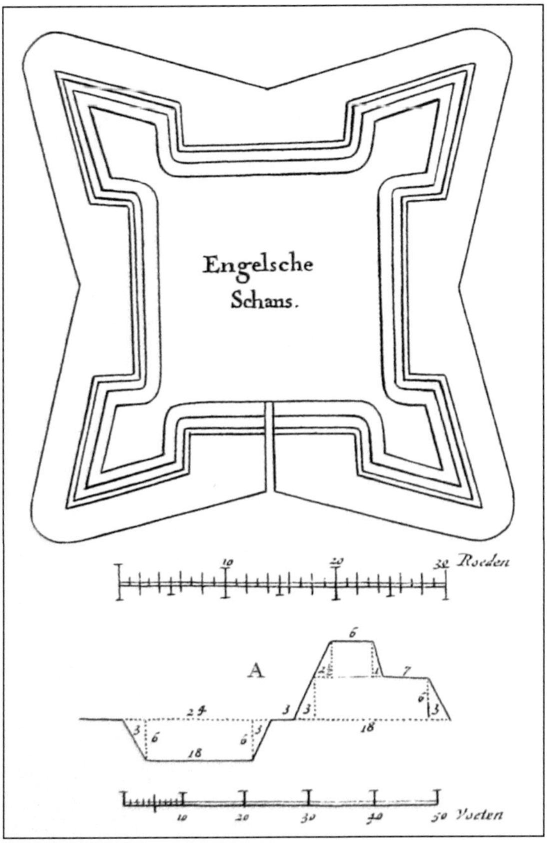

4.11 Hugo de Groot's detail of the 'Engelsche Schans' (English Sconce) at Grol.

Monck would go on to discuss fortress warfare in his *Observations upon Military & Political Affairs*, written between 1644 and 1646 whilst he was a prisoner in the Tower of London.[43]

By 1637, Hexham had already written histories of two other sieges, but it is his *A True and Briefe Relation of the Famous Siege of Breda* (1637) which was the most important for English readers, detailing, as it did, the British role in the siege. Hexham's own experiences convinced him of the important of siegecraft in warfare, promoting the Maurician methods of siegecraft. He explained that by spending a few hundred pounds digging approaches and saps was an effective method of capturing a town and at the same time,

of the Seas, &c. Composed by Henry Hexham, Quartermaster to the Regiment of the Honorable Colonel Goring. Printed at Delft by James Moxon, 1637. Viewed at <http://www.generalmonck.com/hexham-monck.htm> (accessed 16 December 2018).

43 George Monck, *Observations upon Military & Political Affairs*, (London: 1671), pp. 115–42.

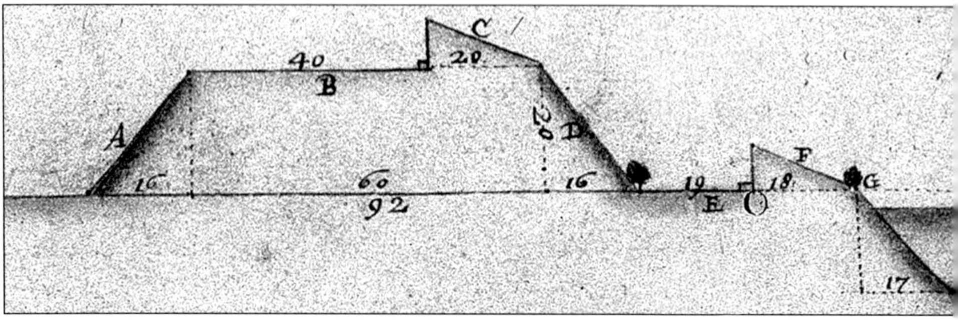

preserving the lives of the besieging soldiers. In this, he predates Vauban's famous maxim of 'Spend more powder and save more blood.' Hexham also considered that establishing secure lines of circumvallation and contravallation was more humane (to both sides) than blockading a town and staving it into submission.

Whilst Hexham was the chief proponent of the Dutch methods of siege warfare, he was certainly not the only one. Robert Ward, most famous for his *Anima'dversions of War*, described the 1624–5 siege, both the Dutch defence and the Spanish methods of attack. Looking at the 1637 siege, Ward considered that Frederick Henry's victory was the result of the calculated study of the siege tactics of his opponents, as well as the application of the rational methods of siegecraft, and a thorough mastering of the complex anatomy of siege operations. Richard Norwood's *Fortification or Architecture Military* of 1639 was an early full-scale work in English on siege warfare, whilst the impact of the Civil Wars in Britain on the development of fortress warfare itself was probably first considered in David Papillon's 1645 *A Practical Abstract of the Arts of Fortification and Assailing*.[44]

However, it was not just in the form of the written word that Breda influenced fortress warfare during the Civil Wars, Monck and Lucas were just two out of a number of British-born soldiers who served at the siege of Breda and would put this experience of Continental fortress warfare to use in sieges, fortress design and garrison duty back in Britain:

- Thomas Fairfax (York in 1644, Leicester, Taunton, Bridgwater, and Bristol in 1645, Oxford in 1646, Wallingford Castle in 1646, and Colchester in 1648)
- Henry Gage (Boarstall House, Basing House, Banbury Castle, Oxford in 1644)
- George Goring (Portsmouth in 1642, Wakefield in 1643, Farnham, Salisbury, Exeter, and Taunton in 1645)
- Charles Lucas (Berkeley Castle in 1645 and Colchester in 1648)
- George Monck (Dundalk in 1647, Edinburgh Castle, Dirleton Castle, Roslin Castle, and Borthwick Castle in 1650, Tantallon Castle, Blackness Castle, Inchgarvie, Burntisland, Stirling Castle, and Dundee in 1651)

44 Black, p. 105 and p. 107.

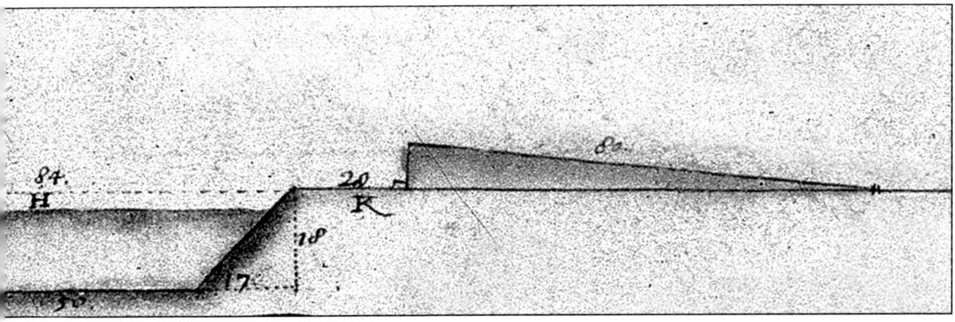

4.12 The profile of the defences at Grolle (Grol). This represents the norm for Dutch fortifications. (With thanks to Godfried Nijs)

- Philip Skippon (who also participated in the 1624–5 siege) (Tower of London in 1642, Gloucester in 1643, and Oxford in 1646. Skippon may also have advised on the construction of London's fortifications in 1642–3)[45]
- Richard Willys (Newark in 1645, and Oxford in 1646)
- Henry Wilmot (Marlborough in 1642)

In addition to these named individuals, there were countless other British soldiers who laboured on fortifications, garrisoned places of strength, and fought at sieges. Undoubtedly, they felt similar to their Dutch contemporaries who considered the status of the pioneer as the ultimate degradation, although they were more willing to dig and carry when offered a bonus of a shilling of a day.[46] Their practical experience would be utilised throughout the British Isles.

In 1636, some 9,300 English and Welsh, and 3,600 were serving in the army of the Dutch States General (representing 17.2 percent of the total of 75,000), whilst the British contingent of the Spanish Army of Flanders was 6,500 (7.5 percent of 87,000).[47] At the siege of Maastricht in 1632, of the officer casualties suffered by the besiegers, 605 were British. During the 1630s, British soldiers were to be found serving in the garrisons of no fewer than 40 Dutch towns, most of which were in a broad diagonal between Doesburg, Nijmegen and Zwolle in the east to Bergen-op-Zoom and Dordrecht in the west, in a chain of fortresses which had largely been constructed between the fall of Antwerp in 1585 to the truce of 1609, creating an identifiable

45 Victor Smith, and Peter Kelsey, 'The Lines of Communication: The Civil War Defences of London', in Stephen Porter (ed.), *London and the Civil War* (Basingstoke: MacMillan Press Limited, 1996), p. 140.

46 Duffy, p. 147.

47 Hugh Dunthorne, *Britain and the Dutch Revolt, 1560–1700* (Cambridge: Cambridge University Press, 2017), pp. 67–9.

war zone,[48] and in the words of the Scottish traveller, William Lithgow, making the Netherlands 'the garden of Mars … and the light of all Europe'.[49]

Elsewhere, during the 1620s, Frankenthal, Heidelberg, and Mannheim were garrisoned by English troops, whilst the garrison of the Danish town of Stralsund, besieged by imperial forces (May to 4 August 1628) included a sizeable Scottish contingent, and Alexander Seaton, Alexander Lindsay, Robert Munro, and Alexander Leslie were either part of the garrison or the relief force. Following the siege:

> Sir Alexander Leslie being made governour, he resolved for the credit of his countrymen to make an out-fall upon the Enemy, and desirous to conferre the credit on his own Nation alone, being his first Essay in that Citie.[50]

Following the siege, Alexander Leslie was appointed governor of Stralsund and was succeeded by another Scot in Swedish service, James MacDougal, in 1630. Less than a decade later, Leslie would go on to capture Edinburgh Castle in what was the first fortress-warfare action of the entire Civil Wars, and later still, would, with Sydnam Poyntz (who had learnt siege tactics in the Netherlands),[51] successfully besiege Newark.

Yet before even the middle of the 17th Century, the Spanish and Dutch, who had for so long dominated siege warfare, were no longer at the cutting edge. The long series of campaigns which had commenced in 1621 lacked the urgency and drive which characterised the first years of the Eighty Years' War, something typified at the siege of Breda in 1624 when a ceasefire was implemented to allow the Polish Prince Ladislaus to inspect the rival lines.[52] In 1654, Henrik Rysensteen highlighted this stagnation in Dutch military engineering, complaining that there were:

> but few alterations of attacks, seeing they are almost all of them made after the same manner … and this proceeds chiefly from the impression which many had, and still have, that the fortifications were at perfection, contrary to the experience and matter of fact in the late wars.[53]

On the Continent, it was no longer necessary to explain the terms of siegecraft (as early as the 1620s, Marolois in his *Art of Fortification* had claimed 'the definitions of Fortification are by the daly use of armes growne common').[54] In 1627, Antoine de Ville became military engineer to Louis XIII, and year later he wrote the influential

48 Dunthorne, pp. 80–1.
49 William Lithgow, *The rare adventures and painful peregrinations of William Lithgow* (1614) (Glasgow, 1906), p. 303.
50 Robert Monro, *His Expedition with the Worthy Scots Regiment called Mac-keyes* (London, 1637), volume 1, pp.77–78.
51 Dunthorne, p. 97.
52 Duffy, p. 104.
53 Henrik Rysensteen, *Versterckte Vesting* (1654), in Duffy, p. 104.
54 Lawrence, p. 342.

Les fortifications… contenans la manière de fortifier toute sorte de places tant regulierement, qu'irregulierement. Such was the importance of this book, it was reprinted in 1640 (and again in 1666), and influenced Vauban. By the late 1630s France was overtaking the Dutch as the pre-eminent experts in fortress warfare. Whilst de Ville's 1639 *De la charge des gouverneurs des places … un abrege de la fortification*[55] must have least been known to British military engineers, French influence was slow to be taken up in Britain, and was probably only first described in 1648 in Gerbier's *Interpreter of Fortification* which had parallel English and French texts on facing pages.[56] but in Britain, Dutch techniques were still the most commonly adopted, and so the demand for treatises was undiminished, including Robert Norwood's *Fortification or Architecture Militas* which appeared in 1639, just as the Bishops' War was breaking out.

At the outbreak of the First Civil War, both the Royalists and Parliamentarians lacked experienced gunners and engineers, and short of homegrown expertise, foreign artillery and engineering experts were employed. The Oxford Army included a number of French gunners in its artillery train, including Monsieur La Riviere, and Monsieur St Martin. Raoul Fleury was Chief Engineer to the train, whilst another Frenchman, Captain Montgarnier[57] was Comptroller. Another Frenchman attached to the Oxford Army's artillery train was Bartholomew La Roche, the King's Master Fireworker. La Roche was one of a number of foreign officers who accompanied Prince Rupert and Prince Maurice to England in September 1642. *The Royalist Ordnance Papers* make several references to La Roche and the materials he used for his 'black art' – various types of incendiary and explosive devices, but chiefly mortar shells, and fire-pikes (pole-type weapons tipped with inflammable materials). The latter were used during the storming of Bristol in July 1643 and caused panic amongst the defenders.[58] La Roche regularly complained about how he was treated and on at least one occasion, threatened to resign. But the award of the knighthood ensured that he remained in Royalist service until the end of the war.[59]

Also accompanying Prince Rupert was the Walloon, Bernard de Gomme, who was later to become Engineer General to Charles II. He played a key role in the storm of Bristol, and then drew improved defences for Chester, Liverpool and Lathom House, and also contributed to the fortifications of Oxford and Newark. But someone who arguably made a greater contribution to Civil War fortifications than de Gomme was, in the words of Lord Digby, 'our excellent engineer' the Swede Dedrich Beckmann.

Beckman probably arrived in England in early 1643. He was commissioned Captain and by a Royal Warrant was appointed Engineer in Ordinary:

55 Black, p. 116.
56 Duffy, p. 146.
57 Ian Roy (ed.), *The Royalist Ordnance Papers, Part 1* (Oxford: Oxfordshire Record Society, 1964), pp. 26–7.
58 Eliot Warburton, *Memoirs of Prince Rupert and the Cavaliers* (London, 1849), Vol. II, pp. 233–64.
59 British Library, *Additional Manuscripts*, MS 18981, f. 212.

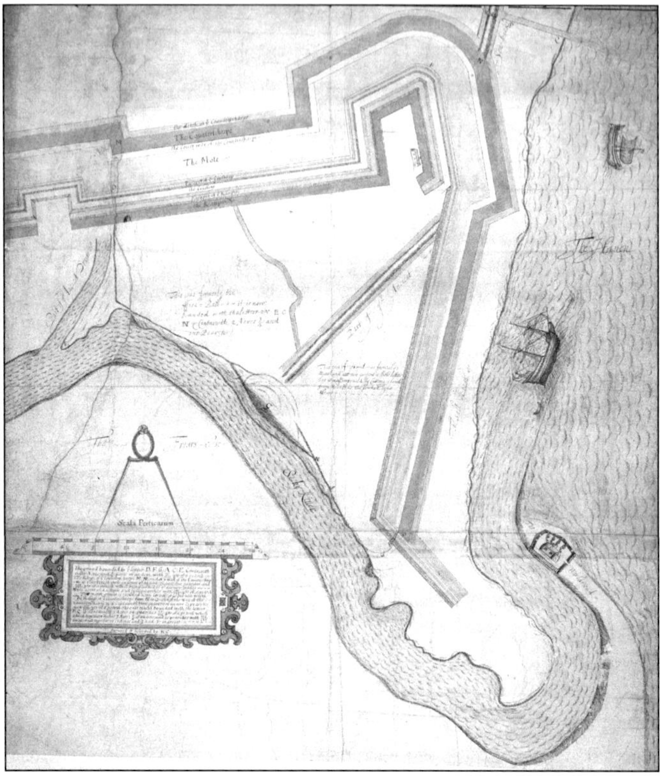

4.13 Richard Clampe's plan of the fortifications near the Boal, South Lynn, between Sechy River and the Haven. (NRO – King's Lynn Borough Archives, KL/C 48/16 (originally BC 21))

> 'Charles by the grace of God King of Great Britain, France and Ireland, Defender of ye Faith etc. To our trusty and wellbeloved Captain Diderich Beckman Greeting. Whereas for the better and more exact fortifying of Our Citty of Oxford and diverse other [towns?] of this Our Kingdom of England We have occasion to make use of many Engineers, knowing therefore that…'[60]

Beckman worked on the defences of Hillesden House and Malmesbury, and most importantly Oxford where his designs represented the most sophisticated urban defensive scheme anywhere in the country. Christopher Duffy considers that Oxford's 'bastion-like salients of the envelope strongly resemble the works at Ostend'.[61]

60 'Engineer in Ordinary in the Royalist Army at Oxford, 1643–5', Draft commission to, Harl. MS. 6804, f.24. quoted by Paul Beckman, '…our incomparable engineer…', 'The English Civil Wars. 1643–45. The fortifications of Oxford, Malmesbury and the fall of Hillesdon House' (unpublished), p. 5.

61 Duffy, p. 150.

Both Prince Rupert and his brother, Maurice, had seen action at the siege of Breda in 1637 (Rupert may first have met the young Bernard de Gomme there).[62] Rupert participated in fortress warfare-type actions at Cirencester, Lichfield, Reading, Bristol, and Gloucester (all in 1643), Chester, Newark, Wigan, Liverpool, and Lathom House (all 1644), and Leicester, and Bristol (both 1645). His brother was at Bristol, Dorchester, Weymouth, Portland, Exeter, Dartmouth Castle, and Plymouth (all 1643), Lyme Regis (in 1644), Chester and Worcester (1645), and Oxford (1646).

Other foreign artillery and engineering experts in Royalist service included Jacques Benoist (a French conductor of the King's ordnance at Oxford), 'Monsieur Gastines' (of unknown origin, but who served the King as a military engineer), the Danish fireworker Andrew Grove, Captain Charles Frederic Shebis (another French engineer), 'Monsieur Hen. Spee, a gentleman of the Ordnance for the King, was possibly French,[63] and a Dutch fireworker by the name of Hendrick who participated at the siege of Bristol in 1643.[64]

Whilst Parliamentarian pamphleteers found something sinister in the 'subtle art of the foreign engineers',[65] it did not prevent overseas experts joining the ranks of the Parliamentarian armies. There was the Dutchman, John Dalbier, who severed first with the Earl of Essex and later conducted the sieges of Donnington Castle and Basing House (Dalbier changed sides during the Second Civil War and was killed at St Neots in 1648). The German, Rosworm, served Parliament in the north of England, fortifying Manchester in 1642, then Liverpool (Rosworm's scheme is included in de Gomme's plan of Liverpool's defences), Preston, and Blackstone Edge. The Scot, James Wemyss, the 'Master Gunner of England', and described on one occasion as 'that excellent engineer', had seen service in the army of Gustavus Adolphus.[66]

The New Model Army List identifies two Dutch engineers: Peter Manteau van Dalem (Engineer general), and Eval Tercene (Engineer chief).[67] Others included the French-born military engineer David Papillon who proposed defensive schemes for both Gloucester and Northampton, and the Dutchman, Cornelius van den Boom who planned the fortifications of the Parliamentarian garrison of Newport Pagnell,[68] a scheme which, alongside those designed by Clampe for King's Lynn, rivalled those at Oxford as the most sophisticated designs of the entire Civil Wars.

In addition to the named foreign experts there are a number of allusions to other, nameless engineers:

62 A portfolio of de Gomme's maps and drawings now in the British Library suggests that a 13-year-old de Gomme may been at Breda in 1637, where he might also have met a 14-year-old Prince Rupert for the first time. Andrew Saunders, *Fortress Builder* (Exeter: University of Exeter Press, 2004), p. 14.

63 Mark Stoyle, *Soldiers and Strangers: An ethnic history of the English Civil War* (Yale: Yale University Press, 2005), pp. 213–221.

64 Ross, p. 33.

65 Duffy, p. 147.

66 Ross, p. 24 and pp. 31–3.

67 Ross, p. 27.

68 Saunders, *Fortress Builder*, pp. 74, 76

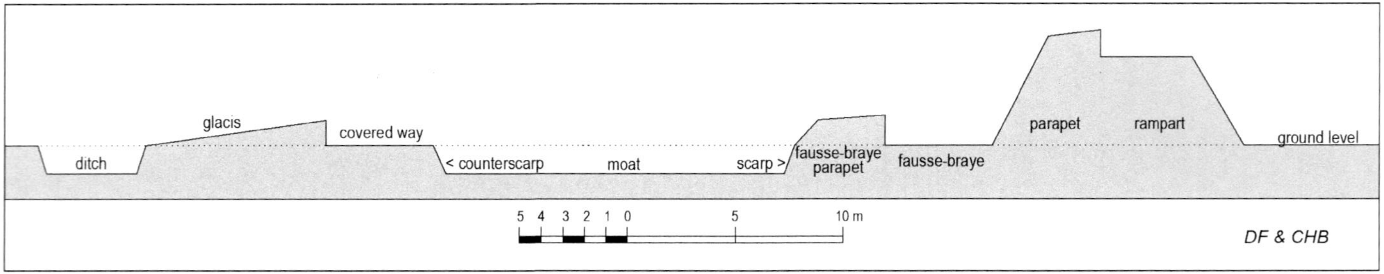

4.14 (above): King's Lynn was one of the very few examples of Dutch practice being implemented in Britain. Here is Richard Clampe's design shown in profile. (Plan by Charles Blackwood, from information provided by David Flintham)

4.15 (below): The British 'norm' is represented here – a simple ditch with the excavated earth being used to build the accompanying rampart. (Plan by Charles Blackwood, from information provided by David Flintham,- and from the British Museum excavation)

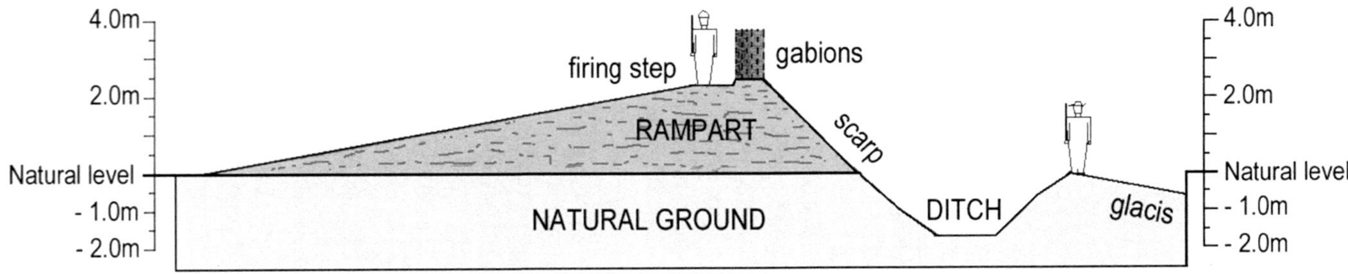

> One foreigner – another account says a Dutchman – was casting at York, in July, 1642, brass mortars for the Royalists; another of his Majesty's engineers in October, 1642, prepared, at Whitchurch, 'divers engines'; a Frenchman reported 'very skilfil', but who nearly succeeded, when manufacturing 'fire works', in blowing up the young princes, in the same year and month; a Dutchman, employed in Exeter, 1642, a 'very good one', was said to have conducted the party which assaulted Southsea Castle in 1642; another, known as 'the Devill with one legge', was employed under Waller, at Arundel, in December, 1643.[69]

The so-called foreign experts did not necessarily all have to have military backgrounds nor were they (initially at least) engaged in military activities. For example, in the years coming up to the outbreak of the war, there was a great deal of interest in the draining of fenlands, and during the 1630s the Earl of Bedford headed a group of landowners, known as the 'Gentleman Adventurers' who invested in a scheme to drain the East Anglian fens, in so doing creating farmland (the investors would be repaid through the grants of land) as well as controlling winter flooding. The Dutch engineer Cornelius Vermuyden (1595–1677) was hired to design and implement a drainage programme (Vermuyden had already worked on projects in Essex and later in Lincolnshire, and been knighted in 1629),[70] and it is likely that Vermuyden bought in Dutch engineers to assist, thus potentially spreading Dutch fortress techniques. The outbreak of the Civil War brought a temporary halt to the work, but during the 1650s, prisoners of war (initially Scots after the battle of Dunbar, and then Dutch during the first Dutch War) were used when work recommenced. Whilst it is not clear what Vermuyden himself did during the wars (he was reappointed to direct the works in 1650), it is possible that one of his nephews served as a colonel in the Army of the Eastern Association). So, there was plenty of opportunity for Dutch engineers to influence fortress construction particularly in East Anglia, whilst a further link with Dutch 'civil' engineering was the use of the term 'trench dyke' to describe a rampart.[71]

There was another aspect of Continental fortress warfare that made it across the Channel, although despite what Parliamentarian propagandists would have posterity believe, the First Civil War was relatively free from the sackings, burning and other atrocities which was a feature of the Thirty Years' War. But notwithstanding the outcry from other senior Royalists, one veteran of the European wars, Prince Rupert, refused to abandon what he saw as the accepted European tactic of the *Brandeschatzung* or 'fire raid', sacking Cirencester in February 1643, and most notoriously, Birmingham on 3 April, which resulted in a widely circulated Parliamentarian account:

> Having thus possessed themselves of the town, they ran into every house, cursing and damning, threatening and terrifying the poore Women most terribly, setting naked Swords and Pistols to their breasts, they fell to plundering all the Towne before them, as well

69 Ross, p. 29.
70 J. Korthals-Altes, *Sir Cornelius Vermuyden* (London: Williams and Norgate, 1925).
71 William Lithgow, *The Present Surveigh At London*, in Ross, p. 81 and p. 82.

> Malignants as others, picking purses and pockets, seeking in holes and corners, Tile of houses, Walls, Pooles, Vaults, gardens and every place they could suspect for money or goods, forcing people to deliver all the money they had … They beastly assaulted many Women's chastity, and impudently made their brags of it afterwards, how many they had ravished; glorying in their shame especially the French among them were outrageously lascivious and lecherous … That night few or none went to Bed, but sate up reveling robbing, and Tyranising over the poor affrighted Women and Prisoners, drinking drinke, healthing upon theire knees, yea, drinking Healths to Prince Rupert's Dog…[72]

Whilst this is Parliamentarian propaganda, it does highlight the horror of the aftermath of the assault which would become ever more familiar throughout the country as the war progressed.

Probably the best known 'atrocity' of the First Civil War occurred on 28 May 1644 at Bolton which was besieged by Prince Rupert. The Parliamentary garrison, under the command of Alexander Rigby, reinforced by some 500 townsmen, had thrown back the initial Royalist assault and had then, in full view of the Royalists, hanged a captured Irish soldier. Understandably enraged, Prince Rupert ordered a second attack which drove the defenders back through the streets to the centre of Bolton (the so-called 'Geneva of the North'), where, according to Parliamentarian accounts, a massacre took place (which Parliamentarian propagandists likened to the sack of the German city of Magdeburg on 20 May 1631 during the Thirty Years' War):

> at theire entrance, before, behind, to the right and lefte, nothing heard but kill dead, was the word in the Towne, killing all before them without any respect … pursuing the poore amazed people, killing, stripping and spoiling all they could meet with nothing regarding the doleful cries of women and children; but some they slashed as they were calling for quarter, others when they had given quarter, many hailed out of their houses to have their brains dasht out in the strettes…[73]

But closer examination of other evidence changes this picture somewhat as some 700 townspeople who had taken refuge in a church were granted quarter which goes along with Prince Rupert's order prior to the second assault that no quarter would be given to 'Any person then in Armes'.[74] According to the contemporary Bolton Parish Registers, 78 townsmen and four townswomen perished, together with several hundred of Rigby's men. By way of comparison, of Magdeburg's 30,000 citizens, only 5,000 are said to have survived. After the sack, the Imperial Field Marshal Gottfried Heinrich Graf zu Pappenheim wrote:

72 Anon., *Prince Rupert's Burning love for England* (London, 1643), p. 25.

73 George Ormerod (ed.), 'Lancashire Civil War Tracts', in *Military Proceedings in Lancashire* (Manchester: Chetham Society, 1884), p. 191.

74 John Barratt, *Cavaliers: The Royalist Army at War, 1642–1646* (Stroud: Sutton, 2004), p. 237.

4.16 Richard Clampe's plan of the 1645–6 siege of Newark (London, 1650). Sophisticated by English standards, but far less so when compared with typical Continental practice.

I believe that over twenty thousand souls were lost. It is certain that no more terrible work and divine punishment has been seen since the Destruction of Jerusalem. All of our soldiers became rich. God with us.[75]

75 Hans Medick and Pamela Selwyn, 'Historical Event and Contemporary Experience: The Capture and Destruction of Magdeburg in 1631', in *History Workshop Journal* (Oxford: Oxford University Press, 2001), no. 52 (Autumn 2001), pp. 23–48.

4.17 Prince Frederick Henry (left) and his cousin Count Ernst Casimir at the siege of 's-Hertogenbosch in 1629. Frederick Henry's capture of a number of cities from the Spanish earned him the nickname 'the conqueror of cities'. (Rijksmuseum, Amsterdam)

The longer the fighting continued, the more vicious it became, and with it, the occurrences of atrocities increased (the Battle of Naseby marks something of a watershed in this respect, whilst there were instances of atrocities prior to Naseby, the sack of Basing House, the siege of Colchester and the Cromwellian campaign in Ireland all occurred after June 1645). But even the 3,500 defenders and inhabitants of Drogheda that Cromwell is said to have butchered, or the citizens of Colchester who succumbed to disease and hunger in what was arguably the worst siege in England are comparatively minor when taken in a European context.

The Civil Wars provided schooling for home-grown engineers, and the longer they went on, home-grown engineers increased in prominence, and, as had been the case a century before, whilst the concepts and influences were still largely foreign, they were increasing being implemented by British engineers. One example of a British engineer who had served his 'apprenticeship' abroad, but would hone his skills at home was Charles Lloyd, a professional soldier from Montgomeryshire. Lloyd had previously seen Dutch service later became Engineer-in-Chief and Quartermaster General to the King. He was responsible for commencing Oxford's fortifications in 1643, a scheme which Beckmann later developed. Another was Henry Sherburne (brother of Edward Sherburne, a Lancashire Catholic, who, as Clerk to the Ordnance at the Tower of London, was imprisoned by Parliament in 1642, but subsequently escaped to Oxford). Sherburne became Chief Engineer of the Oxford Army towards the end of the war. But just before the fall of Oxford in 1646, he was killed by 'tumultating souldiers'.[76] Another Civil War soldier who was influenced by Dutch methods, to the extent that he proclaimed himself an expert in siegecraft and actually had siegeworks cut into his garden at Charborough, was the Parliamentarian Sir Walter Earle. Made governor of Dorchester, he besieged Corfe Castle in 1643. But after six weeks, and having lost in the region of 100 men, he was repulsed and fled in ignominy.[77]

No study of European influences on Civil War military engineering would be complete without mention of England's greatest architect of the first half of the 17th century, Inigo Jones (1573–1652). Heavily influenced by Andrea Palladio, Jones visited Italy, the Netherlands, Germany, Switzerland, and Denmark, and during his travels he must surely have been exposed to Continental fortress design.[78] In 1644 he was sent to Basing House to advise on its fortifications. He took with him three Italian works on fortifications (in two of these, Jones made detailed annotations, suggesting that he was looking to apply these techniques at Basing House). In the third, Gabriello Busco's *L'Architettura Militare* (*c.*1601), he highlighted a section about fortifying hill-sites (of relevance at Basing).[79] Jones was famously captured at Basing House when it fell in October 1645.

There were, of course, some British 'siege experts' with no apparent foreign connections. Richard Clampe, who designed the defences at King's Lynn and later the siegeworks at Newark was one, and another was Thomas Rainborowe. Despite his lack of Continental service, Rainborowe's experience of handling artillery both afloat and on land during the defence of Hull in 1643 proved to be excellent grounding for his later career as Parliament's 'siege-master', during the final year of the First Civil War where he participated in six major and minor sieges in the West Country, and at Colchester in the summer of 1648 during the Second Civil War.[80] Another was Thomas Rudd, who was described as 'Captain Thomas Rudd, engineer to King Charles the First' wrote a supplement on fortification to Elton's 1659 *Complete Body of the Art Military*.[81] In his list of English engineers with no apparent Continental experience, Ross identifies 11, including John Mansfield who served with de Gomme at Bristol in 1645,[82] so he cannot have been the only one to have gained knowledge of siegecraft by serving with foreign experts.

The overwhelming importance of fortress warfare during the 17th century was summed up by Roger Boyle, 1st Earl of Orrery in his *A Treatise of the Art of War*

76 Ian Roy (ed.), *The Royalist Ordnance Papers, Part 2* (Oxford: Oxfordshire Record Society, 1974), p. 444.

77 Duffy, pp. 145–6.

78 It is rumoured (but not corroborated) that in around 1620 the Dutch East (West?) India Company invited Jones to design a fort to protect the harbour of New Amsterdam on the Hudson River. Jones's design was for a stone-built fort.

79 Michael Leapman, *Inigo, The Life of Inigo Jones, Architect of the English Renaissance* (London: Review: an imprint of Headline Book Publishing, 2004), p. 6.

80 Whitney R.D. Jones, *Thomas Rainborowe (c.1610–1648): Civil War Seaman, Siegemaster and Radical* (Woodbridge: Boydell Press, 2005), p. 35, p. 109.

81 Saunders, *Fortress Britain*, p. 72.

82 Ross, pp. 28–9.

4.18 Dating from around a decade after the siege of 's-Hertogenbosch in 1629 (painting attributed to Pieter de Neyn), this view would be typical of any siege of the period. (Rijksmuseum, Amsterdam)

(1677), noting 'we make ware more like foxes than lions; and you will have twenty sieges for one battle.'[83] Despite Orrery having seen action in both Scotland and in his native Ireland, participating in at least three sieges,[84] his assertion was based entirely on Continental examples, feeling that no British siege worthy of consideration. More recently, Christopher Duffy commented, overall 'by Continental standards, the English proved very incompetent in some important branches of siege-work', placing particular emphasis on the lack of skill in which artillery was used.[85] Nowhere in Britain was the Continental practice of the double circumvallation (the outer of the two designed to deter a relieving army) employed: in the face of a relieving force, besiegers would instead either break off the siege and offer battle, or retreat. Even when lines of circumvallation were constructed (such as at Newark and Colchester) they amounted to no more than five kilometres in length, compared to the 18 kilometres of works Prince Frederick Henry encircled 's-Hertogenborsch in 1629.[86] A similar lack of sophistication applies to fortifications where urban fortification in Britain typically resembles European siegeworks rather than urban defences, with only the designs at King's Lynn, Newport Pagnell and Oxford coming close to typical European practice. Writing from a position of experience, having witnessed Civil War fortifications and sieges first hand, Papillon observed:

83 Roger Boyle, 1st Earl of Orrery, *A Treatise of the Art of War* (London: 1677), p. 15.

84 <https://www.libraryireland.com/biography/RogerBoyle.php> (accessed 29/12/2018).

85 Duffy, p. 159.

86 Ronald Hutton and Wylie Reeves. 'Sieges and Fortifications' in John Kenyon and Jane Ohlmeyer (eds.), *The Civil Wars: A Military History of England, Scotland and Ireland, 1638–60* (Oxford: Oxford University Press, 1998), p. 215.

> the greater part of the forraigne Fortifications are not for our imitation, because they require a long time to erect them, and more men than we have, or are able to pay, to maintaine and defend them, and more means to finish them, than we have at this present, the meanes of this Nation having beene exhausted, by this unnaturall warre.[87]

Even with foreign expertise and experience, Britain was generally behind the times, even employing medieval siege tactics on occasion. It was only when it came to mining that Britain was ahead of Continental practice. As the wars progressed, the level of home-grown knowledge grew, to the extent that be the end of the fighting, it was the British engineer, rather than his foreign counterpart who was conducting the majority of sieges. But even after more than a decade of conflict, British influence on European practice was, at best, negligible, and only Malthus enjoyed any prestige abroad, although even he gained his experience on the Continent rather than in Britain. Whilst some British troops who had experienced the British Civil Wars saw service at Dunkirk and Mardyke (1657–8), they were as part of larger foreign forces and not called upon as fortress specialists. And at the Restoration, it was Bernard de Gomme who Charles II would appoint as his to 'engineer-in-chief of all of his castles and fortifications in England and Wales'. So after more than 20 years of Civil War and then military government, come the Restoration, when it came to military engineering, it would again be to a Dutchman that the country would turn.

87 David Papillon, *A Practical Abstract of the Arts of Fortification and Assailing* (London: 1647), quoted in Peter Harrington, *English Civil War Fortifications, 1642–51* (Oxford: Osprey Publishing, 2003), p. 10.

5

English Civil War Colours and Guidons

Their Origins in the Flags of the Thirty Years' War Armies

Stephen Ede-Borrett

Note: references in this chapter to either 'cornets' or 'standards' refer to the flags carried by units of horse; 'guidons' refer to the flags of the dragoons; 'colours' or 'ensigns' are the flags of the companies and regiments of foot.

> The Colonels Colours in the first place is of a pure and clean colour, without any mixture. The Lieutenants Colonels only with Saint Georges Armes in the upper corner next the staff: the Major's the same; but in the lower and outermost corner with a little stream Blazant, And every Captain with Saint George Armes alone, but with so many spots or several Devices as partain to the dignity of their respective places.[1]

This paragraph by Captain Thomas Venn in his book *Military Observations or the Tackticks Put Into Practice*, published in London in 1672, referred back to the pre-Restoration system of the differencing of colours, and is perhaps the most widely known of anything written on the subject of English Civil War colours. This is especially so since it was 'popularised' by being quoted by Brigadier Peter Young in his book *Edgehill 1642*, published in 1967.[2] Although of course the statement was known before 1967, I believe Young's book was probably the first time anyone had

1 Captain Thomas Venn, *Military Observations or the Tackticks put Into Practice* (London, 1672), p.181. Although Venn's work was not published until 1672, as with most such works it echoes back to an earlier age and this section on colours describes the system in use before the Restoration in 1660, and the deliberate alteration of the appearance of English military colours by Charles II.

2 Peter Young, *Edgehill 1642: The Campaign and the Battle* (Kineton: Roundwood Press, 1967).

made a serious study of Civil War colours, albeit brief (I do not believe many people know anything of Venn or his book beyond this one paragraph).[3]

It has long been assumed that this system described by Venn was somehow organically English and that the Scots variants of it were copied from their southern neighbours. I will, however, and perhaps heretically, suggest that what has become known as 'the Venn system' may in fact be the English adaptation of a system already in use in the Thirty Years' War and *possibly* introduced into England from Scotland after the Bishops' Wars rather than vice versa.

Admittedly, the one point about this system that is certainly uniquely English is Venn's 'little stream blazant', more usually today referred to by its heraldic term of a 'pile wavy'.[4] As the mark of a sergeant-major's, or major's, colours this is recorded at least as early as 1633 – that is *before* the Venn system itself was in use, by when it was apparently already accepted as the 'major's device'. However its use as such a differencing device is entirely unknown outside England and did not even come into use in Scotland until after Charles II's Restoration in 1660.[5]

But to come back to the system as described by Venn, the system undoubtedly used by the great majority (although admittedly not all) of English regiments of foot between 1642 and 1660.

In 1624, as Laurence Spring has shown,[6] English regiments of foot still carried colours that resembled, or were effectively actually identical to, those carried during Elizabeth's, and even Henry VIII's, reign. The field of these colours was horizontally striped with, usually although not always, a cross of St George in a canton (as Venn sets out for 'his' colours); the stripes were most commonly straight edged but could occasionally have wavy edges – the problem with the latter is the additional time, and therefore cost, required to make them. Occasionally the cross of St George is recorded as still being overall, as on the Drake Flags of 1633 (see Plate 1), instead of in a canton. This latter stand incidentally already uses the pile wavy for its major's company's colours. The cross overall had been usual during the Tudor period (and returned to being the custom after 1660) and from later evidence it is apparent that the pattern militia colours could lag behind those of the Army by a generation,[7] so the use of an overall cross is easily understood.

3 As a point of interest no officer of this name appears in Malcolm Wanklyn's *Reconstructing the New Model Army, 1645–1663*, two volumes (Solihull: Helion & Company, 2015 & 2016). See also Stuart Reid, *Officers & Regiments of the Royalist Army*, five volumes (Leigh-on-Sea: Partizan Press, nd); Charles Dalton, *English Army Lists and Commission Registers, 1660–1714*, six volumes (London: Eyre & Spottiswoode, 1892).

4 Heraldically a 'pile' is a long wedge shape; a 'pile wavy' is simply the same shape with wavy edges.

5 The Royal Regiment of Foot is the first Scottish regiment recorded as using the device. That regiment, however, was on the English establishment post 1661 but it is probably from this regiment that others of the Scottish Establishment adopted it.

6 Laurence Spring, *The First British Army, 1624–1628 : The Army of the Duke of Buckingham* (Solihull: Helion & Company, 2016), pp.78–81.

7 There are a number of English and Welsh militia colours recorded from 1684 and all have the cross of St George in a canton, not overall. A design that had not been usual in the army since the Restoration in 1660.

What meagre descriptions we have for the colours used during the Bishops' Wars also seem to describe striped colours. For example the colours of the Earl of Essex's Regiment of Foot are described as 'orringe tawney and white' and those of the Earl of Newport's as 'greene and white',[8] descriptions that almost certainly refer to striped colours, probably with a canton of St George, even though this is never mentioned.

Whilst many people, including me, have tried to suggest a differencing system, a regimental design if you like, for these striped colours it seems likely that none actually existed and this simple fact may have been part of the appeal for the adoption of a completely new form of colours by the time that the armies were raised again in 1642.

In that two years between 1639/1640 and the Bishops' Wars and the outbreak of the English Civil Wars in 1642 the Venn system appears not only to have become near enough ubiquitous but, with only slight variants, to have emerged fully formed.[9] The question arises, of course, how likely is it that such a new system would suddenly appear and *be widely accepted and used* when colours of foot had otherwise barely changed in the previous almost century and a half? Especially a system so radically different from what had gone before and seemingly bearing little resemblance?

My answer to that question is that this is highly *unlikely*, and that it is far more probable that the whole concept was simply adopted wholesale from elsewhere. It is not so much the system itself that forces this conclusion as its widespread adoption with no comment from military writers and theorists.

There are a vast number of colours recorded from the armies that fought the Thirty Years' War as the four-volume study by Antje and Jürgen Lucht demonstrates,[10] and these barely cover more than a percentage of the recorded flags. However as even a cursory glance through those volumes will show that whilst many European nations combatant in that war had a more defined regimental system of colours than the striped English system, if indeed you can truly call it a system, none have the intricacy and precision inherent in the Venn system.

None that is until you get to look at the French army. Most vexillologists who look at the colours of the French foot will see a simple regimental system of a plain colonel's company colour, later this would be universally white – it was not so during the Thirty Years' War – with all company colours being identical, simply the regimental colour field with an overall white cross. I will come back to this pattern of French colours of

8 Stephen Ede-Borrett, *Ensignes of the English Civil Wars* (Pontefract: Gosling Press, 1997). The colours of Astley's and Harcourt's regiments are similarly described.

9 The Royalist army, or at least the Oxford Army, seemed to have initially favoured the variant Venn system of the first mark being on the major's company's colours instead of a pile wavy, so the first captain's company's colours bore two marks, etc.

10 Antje & Jürgen Lucht, *Fahnen & Standarten Aus Der Zeit Des Dreissigjährigen Krieges, 1618–1648* (Freiburg: Edition Peterstor, 2011–2016).

foot later, but Plate 2 shows the colours of the Gardes Françaises from a contemporary illustration of 1635 when France entered the Thirty Years' War.[11]

The peacetime establishment of the Gardes Françaises in 1630 was 20 companies: a king's company, a colonel's, a lieutenant-colonel's, a major's, 16 captains' companies. Unfortunately of the senior 20 companies only eight colours are recorded (five colours of the 10 additional companies raised in 1635 for the war are also recorded but these do not follow the pattern of the senior, 'permanent', companies).

If we ignore the first colour, which is recorded as the king's company,[12] and acknowledge the use of a pile wavy for the major's company colours, then the similarity between the colours shown here and the system described by Captain Thomas Venn becomes obvious. What is shown are, from top left:

- The King's Company's colour
- The Colonel's Company's colour
- The Lieutenant-Colonel's Company's colour
- The Major's Company's colour. The crowned 'L' is, of course, the cypher of the King, Louis XIII
- The colours of the First, Third, Fifth and Sixteenth Captains' companies.

In 1635 English colours were still striped without any real regimental style or pattern, as they still were in 1640. The system used by the Gardes Françaises here is simple and elegant and allows for every company to be identified to the regiment whilst being subtly different from each other.

Sadly we have zero information on the details of the colours of the Scots army in 1640 (or in 1644–1646 or in 1648 for that matter) aside from the motto ordered to be carried upon them. However in 1651[13] we know that many Scots regiments were using the Venn system, or a variation of it and it is perhaps not too much of a stretch of the imagination to suggest that perhaps the Scots had been using the system since 1639/1640 and had first introduced it to the British Isles.[14]

11 This plate is an adaptation of one that first appeared to accompany my paper 'The Colours of the Gardes Françaises, 1563–1715' and first published in *Arquebusier: The Journal of the Pike and Shot Society*, Vol. XXXIII/IV (London, 2013), pp.29–35 & pl. 1–4. It is reproduced here with the kind permission of the Society.

12 A 'king's company' was not recorded in the English army until after the Restoration when the senior company of each of the English regiments of Foot Guards (and probably in the Irish Regiment of Foot Guards that was raised in London) was the king's company. Whether the senior company of the Lifeguard of Foot in the Royalist army from 1642–1645 was really known as the King's Company is a moot point but actually seems unlikely.

13 F.F. Fitz Paine Fisher, *A Perfect Registry of all Collours, both Horse and Foot, Taken from the Scotts at Dunbar, 3rd September 1650*, British Library Harleian Manuscript 1460.

14 From Fitz Paine Fisher's manuscript the Scots at Dunbar were using at least four different methods of differencing their colours and whilst the 'Venn system' was apparently not the most common it was evident throughout the army in two different versions. Although it has to be said that at least one of the other systems probably came from Denmark and the 'Cadency system' appears to be uniquely Scots.

It has always been assumed that the Scots had copied the idea from the English armies that they had encountered during the First Civil War. However a large number of Scots had served in the French army, and had of course also formed both the officers and the rank and file of the Garde Écossaise since 1418. It would thus seem perfectly natural for them to have brought the concept back to Scotland when they returned to serve in the armies of the Bishops' Wars or simply remembered the colours of the Gardes Françaises from having served alongside it in the Garde Écossaise and suggested the system when they rallied to the cause of the Covenant. Like England, Scotland had not raised a national army for many years and the Scots regiments raised in 1624 were certainly NOT using a system of differencing of captains' colours.

Despite the apparent logical progression of the Venn system from the French Thirty Years' War Army to the Scots army of the Bishops' Wars to English armies of the Civil Wars it has to be a distinct possibility that the idea actually entered the English armies some other way. However if that were the case then it seems unlikely that it would have permeated both Civil War armies so profoundly by 1642, especially considering the disparity of how the King and Parliament raised their respective armies – it had to have been already well known, at least amongst military men by the summer of 1642. I would stress however that whilst I believe that the system came from France and the Gardes Françaises it is just as possible that it transferred directly into the English armies from there and did not come via Scotland.

Of course whilst the Venn system was undoubtedly used by the vast majority of the regiments of foot during the First Civil War, and probably every regiment of the New Model Army and the post-1646 army, there is at least one other pattern of colours that must have come from the French army.

Again the sudden change from the striped pattern of the pre-Civil War years to the colours that are often recorded and described is simply highly unlikely without some outside influence.

Many colours recorded in contemporary records give no idea of the existence on them of a differencing device as laid down by Venn. Indeed Symonds, in his famed 'Notebook',[15] records some colours of foot with no differencing device, notably the yellow colours of Sir Gilbert Talbot's Regiment of Foot.[16] Coupled with these two facts is the statistic that the numbers of 'lieutenant-colonel's company colours' recorded or captured is far in excess of the one in eight or one in 10 that the universal adoption of the Venn system would indicate.

Given these indicators it would appear that, in line with many Continental armies, some English regiments of foot carried a stand whereby the colonel's company's colours was plain (although they sometimes bore a badge or device from the colonel's family

Stephen Ede-Borrett & Brian McGarrigle, *Flags of the English Civil Wars, Part Two: The Scottish Colours of Foot and Cornets of Horse* (Leeds: Raider Games, 1989).

15 British Library Harleian Manuscript 986.

16 British Library Harleian Manuscript 986, f79v.

arms),[17] the lieutenant-colonel's company's colours added the 'canton of St George' but instead of any differencing device all subsequent colours of the regiment were identical to those of the lieutenant-colonel's company.[18]

This concept may, like the Venn system, have come from France where, as I have indicated, it was the usual practice for the colours of most regiments of foot. Certainly before the Civil War no such 'regimental pattern' of colours existed in England but the idea need not have come from France since many German regiments and Swedish regiments used a similar regimental style of all except the colonel's company colours being either identical or near-enough so. Perhaps the only difference between England and Europe was in the customary use of a white colonel's company colours, widespread during the Thirty Years' War, and even adopted in Scotland by at least 1650, although unknown or at least not used in England.[19]

Like the Venn system this pattern for a stand of colours, this concept if you will, was unknown in England before 1642 and can only have been introduced from the Thirty Years' War armies. However from the colours taken at Dunbar we know that, again, many Scots regiments were using this pattern so perhaps, like the Venn system, the English armies encountered it in 1639/1640? The pattern did not, however, ever become genuinely widespread in England, although it certainly did not die out and was in use so long as company colours were carried.[20]

Having considered the origin of the colours of the regiments of foot it is perhaps also worth looking at the guidons of the regiments of dragoons, at the outbreak of the Civil Wars still the 'mounted infantry' they had started out as some decades earlier.

It is frequently, and I would go so far as to say usually, stated that dragoon guidons followed the pattern and style of the regiments of foot, following essentially a Venn system, albeit sometimes without the canton. This is an idea put forward by Peter Young,[21] which has sadly been accepted uncritically by most authors since. To be fair this certainly seems to be pattern of guidons used in English armies at the start of the Civil Wars, although it was by no means universal even in 1642.[22]

In the German armies fighting the Thirty Years' War, however, dragoon guidons were closer in appearance of design, if not shape, to cornets of horse. It was thus

17 This use of a badge on the colonel's colours became more common as the period progressed, even on the colours of the New Model and post-New Model regiments.

18 That stands of colours like this, with no differencing devices on them, existed during the First Civil War was first suggested to me by Dr Les Prince, to whom I extend my thanks.

19 It is possible that in the 1680s the regiments in Tangier were using white colonel's company colours but the practice was unknown in England and the regiments did not bring the custom home with them.

20 Stephen Ede-Borrett, *The Army of James: The Birth of the British Army* (Solihull: Helion & Company, 2018); 'Les Triomphes de Louis XIV', Bibliothèque Nationale, Paris.

21 Again this was in Young's *Edgehill 1642*.

22 Compare, for example, the guidons of James Wardlaw's Regiment of Dragoons illustrated in British Library Add Ms 5247.

normal for such guidons to carry mottos and devices similar to those of the horse, although examples of each appearing separately are also recorded.

Whilst there are very few guidons recorded from the Civil Wars it does appear that as the war progressed dragoon guidons became more like the cornets of horse. Even the much quoted description of the guidons of Sir Samuel Luke's Dragoon Regiment taken by Prince Rupert can actually be read as referring to a cornet style rather than a Venn 'foot pattern'.

Of course, this evolution or changeover may actually not be a Germanic or Continental influence (incidentally it is definitely not French – French dragoon guidons were of a completely different appearance) and could be seen as some sort of natural evolution as dragoons became more like horse.[23] However it seems more probable that as dragoons were individually incorporated as individual companies into regiments of horse, rather than existing as separate regiments, then they took cornet-like devices to their guidons. But the concept for even this evolution has to have come from somewhere and the Thirty Years' War armies, which so many officers had served in or seen, is the logical origin of the idea of breaking with previous accepted convention.

As with the ideas that I have suggested for the origin of the Venn system of the colours of foot I cannot actually conclusively prove any of this. No one recorded why they had changed the appearance of their guidons or why they had created the new system for the colours of foot. However very few changes or innovations come from nowhere; they are almost always copied and adapted from something that went before and, I suggest, this is all that happened in England between 1640 and 1642. English officers saw something that they thought was better than what they had and copied it and changed it to something even better.

English Civil War flags owe a lot to those of the Thirty Years' War; indeed their very appearance came from France and from Germany. But English Civil War armies adapted and used Thirty Years' War tactics and battle plans, their use of the 500-man 'battalion' came from the Netherlands, even the arguments about cavalry tactics came from what was practice in Sweden or France or Germany – why then should we show any surprise that the design and layout of Civil War military colours should have come from Europe?

With thanks to Dr Les Prince whose comments on an early draft of this paper proved invaluable.

23 The story of Okey's Regiment of Dragoons being the first to make a mounted charge (at Naseby on 14 June 1645) is probably not accurate and there were almost certainly similar actions earlier in the war, particularly from those companies integrated into regiments of horse – a practice not uncommon in both armies.

5.1 Plate 1: The Colours of Sir Francis Drake's Regiment of Devon Trained Bands *c.*1633. All colours have a Crimson field, the cross is white as is the pile wavy. Captains' devices are gold shaded in dark brown. (Author's drawing from the surviving colours in the collection of Buckland Abbey, Devon)

5.2 Plate 2: The Colours of the Standing Companies of the Gardes Françaises, *c.*1635
All colours, except the King's, have a mid to dark blue field. The cross is white and the fleurs de lis are gold. The 'Major's Colour' has a gold 'L' and a proper crown in gold and red. The King's Colour is white with all Arms proper. Although not identified as being from specific companies in the original source, and not being shown in this order, rearranging that order shows an identifiable 'Venn system' of devices. (Author's reconstruction)

Notes on Plates

Plate 1: The colours are, from top left, of the Colonel's (the device, an etoile, is from the Drake Arms), the Lieutenant-Colonel's, the Major's, and the three Captains' companies. The Regiment had only six companies and the captains' devices are from their arms, except for the First Captain, who was brother to the Colonel and seems to have avoided the use of the etoile for whatever reason.

Cf. 'The Drake Colours': Stephen Ede-Borrett. *Arquebusier: The Journal of the Pike and Shot Society,* Vol. XX/2, Farnham 1991, pp.4–5.

Plate 2 : The Colours of the standing Companies of the Gardes Françaises, *c.*1635. (Author's reconstruction)

Although not identified as being from specific companies in the original source, and not being shown in this order, rearranging that order shows an identifiable 'Venn system' of devices.

My interpretation of these eight colours would be that they are from (reading from top left):

The King's Company
The Colonel's Company
The Lieutenant-Colonel's Company
The Major's Company
The 1st Captain's Company
The 3rd Captain's Company
The 5th Captain's Company
The 16th Captain's Company

French authorities consider the last five colours are from the companies newly raised for the war and that their continuance is one of the reasons for the collapse of the differencing system used on the original companies. The increase from twenty to thirty companies making the differencing system impractical.

Cf .'The Colours of the Gardes Françaises, 1563–1715', Stephen Ede-Borrett, *Arquebusier: The Journal of the Pike and Shot Society*, vol. XXXIII/IV, London 2013, pp.29–35, & pl. 1–4.

Index

INDEX OF PEOPLE

INDEX OF PLACES

GENERAL TERMS

The Century of the Soldier series – Warfare c.1618–1721

www.helion.co.uk/centuryofthesoldier

'This is the Century of the Soldier', Fulvio Testi, Poet, 1641

The 'Century of the Soldier' series will cover the period of military history *c.*1618–1721, the 'golden era' of Pike and Shot warfare. This time frame has been seen by many historians as a period of not only great social change, but of fundamental developments within military matters. This is the period of the 'military revolution', the development of standing armies, the widespread introduction of black powder weapons and a greater professionalism within the culture of military personnel.

The series will examine the period in a greater degree of detail than has hitherto been attempted, and has a very wide brief, with the intention of covering all aspects of the period from the battles, campaigns, logistics and tactics, to the personalities, armies, uniforms and equipment.

Books within the series are published in two formats: 'Falconets' are paperbacks, page size 248mm × 180mm, with high visual content including colour plates; 'Culverins' are hardback monographs, page size 234mm × 156mm. Books marked with * in the list above are Falconets, all others are Culverins.

The publishers welcome submissions for this series. Please contact us via email (info@helion.co.uk), or in writing to Helion & Company Limited, Unit 8 Amherst Business Centre, Budbrooke Road, Warwick, CV34 5WE.

Other titles in the Century of the Soldier series

No 1 *'Famous by my Sword'. The Army of Montrose and the Military Revolution* Charles Singleton (ISBN 978-1-909384-97-2)*

No 2 *Marlborough's Other Army. The British Army and the Campaigns of the First Peninsular War, 1702–1712* Nick Dorrell (ISBN 978-1-910294-63-5)

No 3 *Cavalier Capital. Oxford in the English Civil War 1642–1646* John Barratt (ISBN 978-1-910294-58-1)

No 4 *Reconstructing the New Model Army Volume 1. Regimental Lists April 1645 to May 1649* Malcolm Wanklyn (ISBN 978-1-910777-10-7)*

No 5 *To Settle The Crown – Waging Civil War in Shropshire, 1642–1648* Jonathan Worton (ISBN 978-1-910777-98-5)

No 6 *The First British Army, 1624-1628. The Army of the Duke of Buckingham* Laurence Spring (ISBN 978-1-910777-95-4)

No 7 *'Better Begging Than Fighting'. The Royalist Army in Exile in the War against Cromwell 1656–1660* John Barratt (ISBN 978-1-910777-71-8)*

No 8 *Reconstructing the New Model Army Volume 2. Regimental Lists April 1649 to May 1663* Malcolm Wanklyn (ISBN 978-1-910777-88-6)*

No 9 *The Battle of Montgomery 1644. The English Civil War in the Welsh Borderlands* Jonathan Worton (ISBN 978-1-911096-23-8)*

No 10 *The Arte Militaire. The Application of 17th Century Military Manuals to Conflict Archaeology* Warwick Louth (ISBN 978-1-911096-22-1)*

No 11 *No Armour But Courage: Colonel Sir George Lisle, 1615–1648* Serena Jones (ISBN 978-1-911096-47-4)

No 12 *Cromwell's Buffoon: The Life and Career of the Regicide, Thomas Pride* Robert Hodkinson (ISBN 978-1-911512-11-0)

No 14 *Hey for Old Robin! The Campaigns and Armies of the Earl of Essex During the First Civil War, 1642–44* Chris Scott & Alan Turton (ISBN 978-1-911512-21-9)*

No 15 *The Bavarian Army during the Thirty Years*

War Laurence Spring (ISBN 978-1-911512-39-4)

No 16 *The Army of James II, 1685–1688: The Birth of the British Army* Stephen Ede-Borrett (ISBN 978-1-911512-39-4)*

No 17 *Civil War London: A Military History of London under Charles I and Oliver Cromwell* David Flintham (ISBN 978-1-911512-62-2)*

No 18 *The Other Norfolk Admirals: Myngs, Narbrough and Shovell* Simon Harris (ISBN 978-1-912174-22-5)

No 19 *A New Way of Fighting: Professionalism in the English Civil War* Serena Jones (ed.) (ISBN 978-1-911512-61-5)

No 20 *Crucible of the Jacobite '15: The Battle of Sheriffmuir 1715* Jonathan Oates (ISBN 978-1-911512-89-9)

No 21 *'A Rabble of Gentility': The Royalist Northern Horse,* 1644-45 John Barratt (ISBN 978-1-911512-98-1)*

No 22 *Peter the Great Humbled: The Russo-Ottoman War of 1711* Nicholas Dorrell ISBN 978-1-911512-31-8)*

No 23 *The Russian Army In The Great Northern War 1700-21: Organisation, Matériel, Training, Combat Experience and Uniforms* Boris Megorsky (ISBN 978-1-911512-88-2)*

No 24 *The Last Army: The Battle of Stow-on-the-Wold and the End of the Civil War in the Welsh Marches, 1646* John Barratt (ISBN 978-1-912390-21-2)*

No 25 *The Battle of the White Mountain 1620 and the Bohemian Revolt, 1618-22* Laurence Spring (ISBN 978-1-912390-22-9)*

No 26 *The Swedish Army in the Great Northern War 1700–21: Organisation, Equipment, Campaigns and Uniforms* Lars Ericson Wolke (ISBN 978-1-912390-18-2)*

No 27 *St Ruth's Fatal Gamble: The Battle of Aughrim 1691 and the Fall of Jacobite Ireland* Michael McNally (ISBN 978-1-912390-38-0)

No 28 *Muscovy's Soldiers: The Emergence of the Russian Army 1462–1689* Michael Fredholm von Essen (ISBN 978-1-912390-10-6)*

No 29 *Home and Away: The British Experience of War 1618–1721* Serena Jones (ed.) (ISBN 978-1-911628-01-9)

No 30 *From Solebay to the Texel: The Third Anglo-Dutch War, 1672–1674* Quintin Barry (ISBN 978-1-911628-03-3)*

No 31 *The Battle of Killiecrankie: The First Jacobite Campaign, 1689-1691* Jonathan Oates (ISBN 978-1-912390-98-4)*

No 32 T*he Most Heavy Stroke: The Battle of Roundway Down 1643* Chris Scott (ISBN 978-1-912390-99-1)*

No 33 *The Cretan War (1645–1671): The Venetian-Ottoman Struggle in the Mediterranean* Bruno Mugnai (ISBN 978-1-911628-04-0)*

No 34 *Peter the Great's Revenge: The Russian Siege of Narva in 1704* Boris Megorsky (ISBN 978-1-911628-02-6)*

No 35 *The Battle Of Glenshiel: The Jacobite Rising In 1719* Jonathan Worton (ISBN 978-1-912174-97-3)*

No 36 *Armies And Enemies Of Louis XIV: Volume 1 – Western Europe 1688-1714: France, Britain, Holland* Mark Allen (ISBN 978-1-911628-05-7)*

No 37 *William III's Italian Ally: Piedmont and the War of the League of Augsburg 1683–1697* Ciro Paoletti (ISBN 978-1-911628-58-3)*

No 38 *War and Soldiers in the Early Reign of Louis XIV: Volume 1 – The Army of the United Provinces of the Netherlands, 1660-1687* Bruno Mugnai (ISBN 978-1-911628-59-0)*

No 39 *In The Emperor's Service: Wallenstein's Army, 1625-1634* Laurence Spring (ISBN 978-1-911628-56-9)*

No 40 *Charles XI's War: The Scanian War Between Sweden and Denmark, 1675-1679* Michael Fredholm von Essen (ISBN 978-1-911628-00-2)*

No 41 *The Armies and Wars of The Sun King 1643–1715: Volume 1: The Guard of Louis XIV* René Chartrand (ISBN 978-1-911628-60-6)*

No 42 *The Armies Of Philip IV Of Spain 1621-1665: The Fight For European Supremacy* Pierre Picouet (ISBN 978-1-911628-61-3)*

No 43 *Marlborough's Other Army: The British Army and the Campaigns of the First Peninsular War, 1702–1712* Nicholas Dorrell (ISBN 978-1-911628-40-8)*

No 44 *The Last Spanish Armada: Britain And The War Of The Quadruple Alliance, 1718-1720* Jonathan D. Oates (ISBN 978-1-911628-01-9)*

No 45 *'Britain Turned Germay:' The Thirty Years' War and its Impact on the British Isles 1638–1660* Serena Jones (editor) (ISBN 978-1-911628-01-9)